THE INDEPEN ___ ГО
DISNEYLAN

GIOVANNI COSTA

Contents

Introduction

2017

The resort celebrates its 25th anniversary in 2017 with a big celebration.

Disneyland Paris is Europe's most popular destination, having amassed over 300 million visitors in 25 years.

The project for the resort started in the 1980s when Disney executives wanted to bring the magic of Disney theme parks to Europe where the original stories, which inspire many Disney fairy tales, originated.

They soon decided on constructing the resort in France due to its central location and favourable weather when compared to some countries further north in Europe.

The fact that the location was less than a two-hour flight from many European locations sealed the deal - and the French government promises to build a lot of infrastructure to guarantee the success of the resort.

Disneyland Park opened in 1992 as a European recreation of California's Disneyland. Its design was, however, updated to reflect the local culture and to take advantage of all the land the company had purchased.

In 2002, Walt Disney Studios Park became the second park at the resort, providing a portal for movie fanatics.

As well as the two theme parks, guests can enjoy the free admission Disney Village area – here you will find shopping and dining experiences that cover a wide range of tastes.

A golf course, a camp-site with an adventure playground, and six themed hotels are also on site.

Disneyland Paris is not just a theme park or a place to ride roller coasters. Guests can meet characters, watch shows and parades, make new friends and enjoy an ambiance that no other theme park resort in Europe rivals. Thrill seekers may not find the tallest and fastest rides in Europe at the resort, but the quality of the experiences offered is second to none.

2017 is a fantastic time to visit as the resort celebrates its 25th anniversary with new rides and shows.

Disneyland Paris is a place where dreams really do come true for guests every single day, and you are about to become one of them.

Planning

Planning a trip to Disneyland Paris may seem daunting. You have to think about transport, accommodation, food, park tickets, spending money, and more. This section aims to get you prepared by following the steps below. All of these steps are further developed in the chapters that follow.

1 Transportation

Decide how you want to get to the resort – will you be flying, driving or taking a train? If you will be using public transport, be sure to check what time you will arrive at the resort and when you will be leaving, so that you can plan your days accordingly.

2 Tickets

If you can, decide whether you will be going back more than once in the next year. If you will be, then consider getting an annual pass instead of buying park entry tickets. There is more information on annual passes later in this book. If an annual pass is not for you, consider what park ticket you want.

3 Accommodation

Decide whether you want to stay on-site or off-site. With on-site packages you get your hotel stay and park tickets for one all-inclusive price. Staying off-site usually means paying for a non-Disney hotel and park tickets separately. This may work out being better for you if you do not plan on visiting the theme parks every day.

4 Park Maps

Towards the end of this guide book we have included exclusively commissioned, easy to read maps. Combine the park maps with the details in this book and decide which attractions and shows you want to visit. Circle the ones you definitely want to visit on your map, or write them down. Knowing which park each of the attractions is in, as well as what area of the park they are located, is essential to making the most of your visit. You do not have to memorise the map, but looking at it in advance will save you valuable time once you arrive.

❺ Check Park Hours and Show Times

Park opening hours vary wildly, the parks can open as early as 8:00am and close as late as 1:00am on certain days of the year. The latest hours are on the Disneyland Paris website at *www.disneylandparis.co.uk/calendars/park-hours/*

Be sure to download the Times Guide that tells you when the parades and shows are taking place, and the locations and times the characters are set to appear. The schedule for your trip can be seen up to two weeks in advance here: *www.disneylandparis.co.uk/entertainment/shows-and-parades-in-disneyland-parks*.

❻ Refurbishments

As Disneyland Paris is open 365 days a year, it does not set aside a period of the year to close and perform its maintenance like most other theme parks do. Instead, Disneyland Paris closes certain rides for refurbishment throughout the year. This is done once a year per ride, usually during periods of low attendance to limit the impact on guests.

Refurbishments are published a couple of months in advance. If there is a particular attraction you want to experience, make sure to check out the refurbishment schedule on our website: www.independentguidebooks.com/dlp/refurbs.

❶ Reading

Read through the whole of this guide thoroughly, bookmarking key pages. Be sure to check our website www.independentguidebooks.com/dlp/ before leaving.

INDEPENDENT GUIDE TO
DISNEYLAND PARIS **2017**

❼ Plugs and Euros

If you are travelling from outside Continental Europe, be sure to bring plug adapters, as sockets in France may differ from your home country.

Also, be sure you get your Euros in advance. Do not rely on buying currency at the airport or train station. We recommend getting a pre-paid currency card that you can top up.

For UK users, we recommend FairFx's service. There is usually a £9.95 fee for the card but by using our special link you can get the card for free: http://bit.ly/debitdlp.

Getting There

Traveling to Disneyland Paris is simple due to its central location. Options include driving, flying and high-speed trains.

Plane

Flying to Paris is convenient for many visitors as the French capital is under two hours away from most of Europe and in the era of budget airlines, flying doesn't have to break the bank either. Paris has three airports you fly into:

Charles-de-Gaulle Airport
This is the main Parisian airport and the largest.

o *By High-Speed TGV Train*: From the airport, get a direct TGV train which takes between 9 and 12 minutes from *Terminal 2* to *Marne-La-Vallee – Chessy (Disneyland)* station. We recommend that buying tickets at the airport to avoid missing pre-booked trains. You can also pre-book online at www.voyages-sncf.com. Tickets are €20 to €25 per person each way. The first train is at about 7:00am; there are no direct TGV trains after 21:19 (check the schedule online by doing a test booking).

o *By Local RER Train*: Get the RER B to *Chatelet les Halles* station, then switch to RER A to *Marne La Vallée – Chessy*. This costs €17.05 per adult with a travel time of about 1 hour 30 minutes. Children under 10 years of age pay €10.50, and children under 4 travel free.

o *By Coach*: The Magical Shuttle bus goes between the airport and Disneyland Paris and even to many Val d'Europe hotels. There are 13 to 14 journeys in each direction daily. Pricing is €20 per adult each way and €16 per child ages 3 to 11. The journey takes about 1 hour and 35 minutes each way. Book at magicalshuttle.co.uk.

o *By Taxi*: A taxi costs €90 to €100 each way for four people. This is the cheapest and most convenient option for large groups.

Orly Airport
Paris' second largest airport.

o *By Coach*: The Magical Shuttle bus is €20 per adult each way, children pay €16. Coach transfers take approximately 1 hour and 35 minutes each way. Book at magicalshuttle.co.uk.

o *By Local RER Train*: Get the *Orlyval* train (6:00am to 11:00pm) to *Antony Orlyval* station. From *Antony Orlyval*, take the RER B to *Chatelet-Les Halles* station. From here, get the RER A to *Marne la Vallée – Chessy (Disneyland)* station. The total journey time is about 1 hour and 30 minutes. Price: €19.25 per adult and €14.25 per child.

o *By Taxi/Private Van*: Prices are €80 to €135 for parties of 3 to 8 people.

This is the cheapest and most comfortable choice for groups.

Beauvais-Tille Airport
This airport is not in Paris, despite the way it is marketed by airlines. Avoid it due to the long transfers.

o *By Public Transport*: Get a shuttle bus from *Beauvais Airport* to *Porte Maillot* bus station. This is €17 one-way (1 hour 15 minutes). At *Porte Maillot*, follow the signs to the Metro and take the Metro Line 1 (yellow) to *La Defense* (10 minutes). At *La Defense* take the RER A line (red) to *Marne La Vallée – Chessy Disneyland* station (50 to 60 minutes – €7.60 per adult, €3.80 per child). This is a long journey, but it is doable. The total journey time is about 2 hour 30 minutes, plus transfer time and the total cost is about €25 per person.

o *By Taxi*: The taxi fare is approximately €180 to €200 each way. We would recommend renting a car in this case instead of using a taxi. The journey is 126km each way, or about 1 hour 30 minutes.

Train

The Eurostar is the easiest option for people from the south of the UK, reaching the doorstep of Disneyland Paris direct in just 2 hours 42 minutes from London, and even less from Ebbsfleet and Ashford. Prices start at £72 (€88) per adult return.

Direct from the UK:
There is one direct train per day that leaves London at 10:14 and arrives at 14:02 at *Marne la Vallée-Chessy* Station (Disneyland).

Return direct trains depart Disneyland Paris at either 17:07 or 18:02 depending on the day of the week. There are no direct trains on Tuesdays and Saturdays, except during British school holidays.

The direct Eurostar service is incredibly convenient with security, immigration and check-in usually over in less than ten minutes.

Eurostar is currently in the process of refurbishing all of its old trains and is introducing brand new "e320" trains. Upgrades will include new interiors and free Wi-Fi throughout the train.

Indirect via Lille:
As there is an only one direct Eurostar service per day, you want to use the indirect option, which gives you more flexibility for times, and can also be cheaper than the direct train.

Passengers board a Eurostar train in the UK (usually with the destination of Brussels) and disembark at *Lille Europe* station, which is about 1 hour and 20 minutes from London. At *Lille Europe*, passengers wait for their connecting TGV train from *Lille Europe* to *Marne la Vallée - Chessy* Station (Disneyland). The whole journey takes as little as 3h03m from London with a 28-minute stopover.

The Eurostar website will not usually show indirect trains more than 12 weeks in advance.

Changing trains is easy to do and 30 minutes is plenty of time. Just check that you are on the right train on the platform, as there may be multiple trains on the same platform at the same time.

The TGV train from *Lille - Europe* makes several stops and only stops at *Marne-La-Vallee - Chessy (Disneyland)* for a few minutes so make sure you do not miss your stop as it is not the end of the route.

There is a very helpful video to this process available from DreamTravelGroup called "Eurostar to Disneyland Paris changing at Lille... no problem!" You can find this video here: http://bit.ly/dlplille.

TOP TIP

Do not book your Eurostar travel with Disneyland Paris as part of a package without checking prices direct with Eurostar. It often works out significantly more expensive to book transportation with Disneyland Paris. We usually recommend you book your train direct at www.eurostar.com. However, when Disney has an offer such as free travel for children, it can be significantly cheaper to book with Disneyland Paris. As such, we recommend you check both options.

You can book Eurostar trains between 3 and 6 months in advance, depending on the season and route.

Eurostar + RER (via central Paris):

Disneyland Paris is about 32km from central Paris, and the city centre is connected to the theme park by the fast and frequent RER train service.

Therefore, you can easily get a high-speed international train to Paris, followed by a local RER train to Disneyland Paris.

This offers you a lot of flexibility – for example, there are up to 18 Eurostar departures per day from London to Paris.

When you arrive at *Paris – Gare du Nord* station by Eurostar, it will take a further 50 to 60 minutes to reach Disneyland Paris.

At the time of writing, a ticket on the Paris RER train from *Gare du Nord* to *Marne-La-Vallée (Disneyland Paris)* costs €7.60 per adult and €3.80 for a child under 10 years old.

Follow the signs at *Gare du Nord*, to the 'Metro and RER' trains.

Take the RER B line in direction of *Robinson, Antony* or *Saint Rémy-lès-Chevreuse* for one stop to *Chatelet-Les Halles*. Here you transfer to RER A by walking to the other side of the platform and getting a train in the direction of *Marne La Vallée – Chessy*.

Use the overhead information boards to verify that the train is going to *Marne La Vallée – Chessy station* (your destination). If it will, there should be a light illuminated next to the station's name. *Marne La Vallée - Chessy (Disneyland)* is the last stop on the RER A line. This journey takes about 40 minutes

DISNEY EXPRESS

If you have booked your train as part of a package, you will have the Disney Express luggage transfer service included. This allows you to drop off your bags at the train station and make the most of your time in the parks.

At *Marne-La-Vallee* Station, follow the signs to the Disney Express counters on the top floor (8:00am to 9:30pm daily).

Here, you check in for your hotel, receive park tickets, meal vouchers (if ordered) and other bits. Leave your bags with the Cast Members at these desks and they will be taken to the luggage storage area in your hotel. Now, explore the parks!

This service is available on both direct and indirect Eurostar services, as well as for guests arriving via TGV at *Marne La Vallée - Chessy* station.

Driving

You have two options to reach Disneyland Paris if driving from the UK.

The Eurotunnel is a specially designed train travel service that allows passengers and vehicles to travel together from Folkestone (England) and arrive in Calais (France) in 35 minutes.

Alternatively, you can take your car on the ferry from Dover (England) to Calais (France). P&O Ferries is a popular company. The ferry crossing is often cheaper than the Eurotunnel but it also takes about 90 minutes, almost three times as long.

From Calais (France) it is a three-and-a-half hour drive to Disneyland Paris. Take the A26 towards Arras passing through St. Omer.

There, take the A1 (also known as *Autoroute du Nord* or E15) towards Paris. Take exit 6 after Charles de Gaulle Airport, onto the A104. This will take you to the A4, follow this road. Exit 14 is Disneyland.

This 290km (180 mi) journey will cost approximately €18 in tolls and approximately €30 in fuel each way.

Hotels

Disneyland Paris owns and operates seven on-site resort hotels, each themed to a part of America – one is even a campsite where you can stay in log cabins. When booking a hotel stay directly with Disneyland Paris, your hotel price will include your park entry tickets.

Advantages of staying at a Disneyland Paris hotel:
• A front desk staffed 24 hours a day
• Friendly Cast Members with knowledge of the resort
• Make dining reservations in person without needing to leave your hotel
• The option to pre-pay for all your meals at the hotel and/or the theme parks.
• Detailed theming and total immersion
• A stay in the heart of the Disney magic
• Extra Magic Hours available daily. EMHs allow hotel guests entry into selected parts of Disneyland Park two hours before other guests, meaning that attraction wait times are either very short or non existent.
• Walking distance to the theme parks: 20 minutes or less.
• Free shuttle service from all the hotels to the theme parks (except Disney's Davy Crockett Ranch)
• The opportunity to meet Disney characters at the hotel throughout your stay.
• Disney Shopping Service: If you buy merchandise in the parks before 3:00pm, you can have it delivered to your hotel to be collected in the evening, leaving your hands free.
• Park admission tickets are included in all reservations unless otherwise stated.

Pricing:

When booking your hotel, your arrival date determines the price for your entire stay (e.g. If you arrive on a date within the Value pricing season and the remaining days of your holiday are in the Moderate pricing season, your whole stay will be charged at the Value price). However, this can also work against you where your arrival date could be in High season and then your other nights in the Regular season. In this case, you will pay the High season rate for the entire duration.

There are two solutions: change your dates, or book one package for the more expensive night(s) and then another package for the cheaper remaining night(s). You may have to leave your room and re-check in if you do this. If you book two back-to-back stays, ask the Cast Member checking you in if you can keep the same room.

To see what season you will arrive in, download the brochure from www.disneylandparis.com. A booking agent may be able to advise what the best option for you is if you book over the phone.

MORE ON PRICING

Room prices in this section are based on arrivals between March 2017 and March 2018. Prices listed are per night and include park tickets for all days of your stay, including check in and check out days.

Prices are per person per night for a standard room based on two adults sharing; so 2 adults will need to double the price per night. A single adult in a room will need to pay a nightly supplement. Additional adults after the second pay a nightly surcharge.

Children under 7 always stay free; children 7 to 11 pay an additional nightly charge, but there may be a sale where this fee is waived for kids.

Multiple night stays carry a lower "per night" cost. The per-night cost after the third night is 45% to 85% cheaper, as most visitors will not need more than four days to visit the resort. This can make a longer stay at the hotels much better value for money overall.

Magic Card:

The Magic Card is exclusive to the seven Disneyland Paris operated hotels, and is given to guests at check-in.

It allows you entry to the theme parks during Extra Magic Hours, access to the hotel pools, and free parking both at the hotel and the theme park parking lot, as well as acting as your room key and meal plan voucher. Not all features may be active at all hotels as the system is being deployed.

During check-in you can also link a credit or debit card to your Magic Card, which will allow you to pay for food and merchandise at most resort locations using the Magic Card instead of paying with your own card or in cash each time. You then settle the bill when checking out and pay one lump sum. This can be a good option for guests from non-euro counties whose credit banks charge a per-transaction foreign currency fee. Just be sure to monitor your spending so as to not go over budget.

Note: Some small stalls (such as those selling drinks or popcorn) do not accept the Magic Card or credit/debit cards, only cash. Restaurants in Disney Village are not operated by Disney, so are unlikely to accept the Magic Card – but do ask.

How to book your stay:

We recommend booking Disneyland Paris hotels or packages through the official website at www.disneylandparis.com.

The website offers you several room types, but suites must be booked over the phone. Both the Disneyland Paris website and phone reservations charge a £16 booking fee.

Disneyland Paris regularly runs promotions with savings of 10-50% off the regular price, or 'get free nights' when you book a stay. If there is not a sale when you are thinking of booking, we recommend you wait as sales run throughout the entire year.

Offers vary seasonally and between different countries. These can be anything from 'free hotel, park tickets and transport for under 12s' to 'free half board meal plans', or even 40% or 50% off. A minimum stay of two or three nights usually applies to promotions, as well as date restrictions.

Booking Tips

Tip 1: You can book Disneyland Paris (and partner) hotels over the phone. Phone booking allows you to pay in instalments instead of one lump sum, with no interest. This allows you to modify your booking up until you have paid the full amount. So, if a better offer becomes available after you book, you can make changes until the final balance is paid, such as upgrading your hotel or adding meal vouchers.

Tip 2: Disneyland Paris runs different promotions in different areas of Europe simultaneously. The good news is you can book any of the promotions from any country. Visit www.disneylandparis.com - at the top of the page select another country, and then try booking through there. You will pay in the currency local to that country. The website's language may also change when you do this. You can also do this by calling Disneyland Paris directly and stating the offer you would like to use.

Here is an example of the different promotions available at the time of writing this guide. The UK Disneyland Paris website offered 30% off stays, the German website offered a €200 discount off stays, the Italian website offered 20% off stays, the US website offered 1 day and night free, and the Spanish website offered 15% off stays plus free meals. Clearly, these are all very different offers with different savings depending on your needs.

Disneyland Hotel

This 565-room, 27-suite, Art Deco/Victorian Hotel is the height of luxury at Disneyland Paris. It is located right at the entrance of Disneyland Park and just 3 minutes away from the Studios.

The Disneyland Hotel is the most expensive and luxurious place to stay on Disneyland Paris property.

The hotel adorns the entrance of Disneyland Park, with the park's turnstiles located underneath it. Some of the rooms have views over Disneyland Park, or over the Fantasia Gardens area in front of the hotel.

The hotel has numerous dining options, including a buffet restaurant (Inventions), an upscale dining experience (California Grill) and a bar (Cafe Fantasia).

From California Grill, you can watch Disney Illuminations from the balcony if you time your dinner right.

The hotel also has the Celestia Spa, which is open from 2:00pm to 9:00pm daily. Facials start at €80, body treatments from €90, manicures and pedicures from €80, and full packages from €120. Reservations are recommended and can be made in person or by calling 6605 from hotel room phones.

In addition to the standard Fastpass service available with every Disneyland Paris park ticket (more on this later in the guide), all guests of this hotel get one Disneyland Hotel Fastpass voucher per day, which allows them instant entry into one Fastpass attraction per day. The Hotel Fastpass is valid all day, except 1:00pm to 4:00pm, and must be surrendered upon use.

Guests staying in the Disneyland Hotel's Castle Club or suites get one VIP Fastpass per person valid for their entire stay. It allows unlimited any-time entry into every Fastpass attraction at both parks.

Castle Club rooms are club level and offer numerous benefits. Castle Club guests may access a private bar area with complimentary non-alcoholic beverages throughout the day, and a perfect view of Disney Illuminations through the windows with the music piped in.

There are also characters present in the morning and sometimes the evening at the Castle Club. There is even a private lift from the Castle Club directly to the turnstiles without needing to walk through the rest of the hotel. This is a truly unique, premium experience.

A 'Princess for a Day' experience is available for

all guests, including those not staying at the hotel. For a charge your little girl can be transformed into a princess with a dress, make-up, accessories and more. Make up and hairstyle only is €50, the dress is an extra €50.

The Club Minnie Playroom is open from 2:00pm to 9:00pm, with activities for children. The games room/arcade is open from 8:00am to 1:00am.

At this hotel, you can have a side profile silhouette cut-out made of your face by an artist. You can also add a Disney character if you would like. Prices range from €10 to €40. This takes place in front of the hotel's shop. The artist is usually present from Wednesday to Sunday between 4:00pm and 10:00pm.

Room size: 34m^2 for standard rooms (up to 4 people, plus one child under 3 years old in a cot), and 58m^2 in the Castle Club Suites (other suites go up to 187m^2 – including the Sleeping Beauty suite, the Cinderella suite, Tinker Bell suite and Walt's Apartment Suite). Family rooms (up to 5 people with one on a sofa bed), and Castle Club rooms (up to 4 people – phone bookings only) are also available.

Breakfast: Extra charge. £23 per day per adult and £21 per child if pre-booked.

Room Prices: 1 night is €429 to €716, 2 nights is €747 to €1320, 3 nights is €1069 to €1929. Additional nights are between €282 and €569. A Castle Club room is priced at an additional €160 to €250 per person per night.

Activities: An indoor pool, sauna, steam bath and a fitness suite are all complimentary for guests. A spa with a massage service is available for an extra fee. A "Club Minnie" Playroom, children's corner, and a video game arcade are also available. Dry cleaning is available at a surcharge.

Extras: Free Wi-Fi is available throughout the hotel, including guests' rooms.

DINING:

Inventions – Buffet service. Lunch with Disney characters from 12:30pm to 3:00pm (Adults: €65, drinks not included; Children: €35 with one drink included). Dinner with Disney characters is from 6:00pm to 10:30pm daily (Adults: €65, drinks not included; Children: €35 with one drink included). Additionally, a themed Brunch is served with the Disney Characters from 1:00pm to 3:00pm every Sunday (Adults: €70, Children: €35). Selected offerings at this restaurant are included in the Premium Meal Plan and the Hotel Meal Plan.

California Grill – Table Service. Starters are €19 to €29. Main courses are €40 to €66. Desserts are €18 to €26. Set menus vary from €79 to €120 for adults; €30 for children. Wines priced €33 to €95. Disney states, "Proper attire [is] required." Open for dinner only between 6:15pm and 10:30pm. Some offerings at this restaurant are on the Premium Meal Plan.

Café Fantasia – Hotel Bar, serving drinks and snacks.

Disney's Hotel New York

This Art Deco, New York themed hotel features 565 rooms and 27 suites, and is a mere 10-minute walk to the parks. A shuttle bus is also available.

Themed to resemble an apartment block in the Big Apple, this is the second closest hotel to the parks, and is located by the entrance of Disney Village and Lake Disney.

Room size: 31m² in standard rooms (for 4 people). Empire State Club lodging includes Club Rooms and Club Suites (ranging between 56m² and 166m², bookings by phone only).

Breakfast: Extra charge. £19 per day per adult and £18 per child if pre-booked.

Room Prices: 1 night is €269 to €429, 2 nights is €426 to €746, 3 nights is €588 to €1068. Extra nights are €122 to €282. For Empire State Club rooms, add an extra €70 to €80 per person per night.

Activities: Complimentary heated outdoor and indoor pools, sauna and/or steam bath, tennis courts and gym. Massages are available for a fee. There is an on-site hairdresser available to hotel and non-hotel guests. A kids' play area and a games arcade are available.

Extras: Free Wi-Fi access is available throughout the hotel, including rooms. Dry cleaning is available. Suite guests get one VIP Fastpass per person valid for their stay, with unlimited entry into every Fastpass attraction without time restrictions.

DINING:

Manhattan Restaurant – Table Service. Main courses are €21 to €33. Set menus are €36 to €56 for adults, and €30 for kids. Some options are included in the Premium Meal Plan and the Plus Meal Plan.

Parkside Diner – Continental breakfast is available. Dinner buffet (18:00 to 23:00) is €35 for adults without a drink, and €19 for kids with one drink. The buffets are on both the Hotel and Plus Meal Plans.

New York City Bar – Bar. Snacks from 11:30am to 3:00pm including sandwiches for €12.50 and pasta salads for €13.

Disney's Newport Bay Club:

This New-England style hotel's 1093 rooms and 13 suites have just come out a multi-year refurbishment. It is a 15-minute walk to the parks, or a free shuttle bus journey away.

Themed to New England, this nautical-inspired hotel houses two restaurants and anchors one end of lake Disney. It is the fourth closest hotel to the parks and has recently come out of a long refurbishment meaning it feels almost brand new inside.

Room size: Standard rooms are 27m²; family rooms for up to 6 guests are also available. Suites include Admiral's Floor at 27m², Honeymoon Suites from 50m² to 63m², The Resort Suite at 55m² and the Presidential Suite measuring 84m².

Breakfast: Extra charge. £19 per day per adult and £18 per child if pre-booked.

Room Prices: 1 night is €269 to €429, 2 nights is €426 to €746, 3 nights is €588 to €1068. Extra nights are €122 to €282. For Compass Club rooms, add an extra €70 to €80 per person per night.

Activities: Indoor and outdoor pools, with deckchairs; sauna/steam bath; and fitness suite. Massages are an extra charge. There is an indoor kids play area.

Extras: Free Wi-Fi access is available throughout the hotel and in guest rooms. This hotel has a convention centre. Dry cleaning is available at a surcharge.

Guests staying in one the suites (not Compass Club) get one VIP Fastpass per person valid for their stay. This allows unlimited entry into every Fastpass attraction. Guests in the Compass club get one Hotel Fastpass per day, allowing immediate entry to the Fastpass queue line to one attraction, except between 1:00pm and 4:00pm.

DINING:

Yacht Club – Table Service. Main courses are €41 to €56. Adult set menus are €47 to €56, €20 and €33 for kids. Some meals are in the Premium & Plus Meal Plans.
Cape Cod – Buffet. €33 for adults with no drinks, €18 for children with one drink. Some meals at this restaurant are in the Premium and Plus Meal Plans.
Fisherman's Wharf – Hotel Bar, serving drinks and snacks.

Disney's Sequoia Lodge

Recreating the ambiance of the American National Parks, the Sequoia Lodge's 1011 rooms and 14 suites are a 15-minute walk from the parks. A shuttle is also available.

Disney's Sequoia Lodge is our favourite on-site hotel.

It is a mid-priced hotel, but it is slightly closer to the parks than the more expensive Newport Bay Club Hotel. In addition, of all the hotels it is the one that we feel immerses guests the most in the theming. There is nothing better than snuggling up next to huge fireplace in the Redwood Bar and Lounge in the winter.

Room size: 22m² in a standard room. Golden Forest Club rooms (with a private lounge with snacks) are also available, as are Honeymoon Suites and Hospitality Suites (55m²).

Breakfast: Extra charge. £15 per day per adult and £13 per child if pre-booked.

Room Prices: 1 night is €235 to €373, 2 nights is €359 to €635, 3 nights is €487 to €901. Additional nights are €88 to €226. Golden Forest rooms are an extra €40 to €60 per person per night.

Activities: Indoor and outdoor pool; fitness suite; sauna/steam bath. Massages are available for an extra charge. Kids play areas are also available.

Extras: Free Wi-Fi access throughout the hotel, including in rooms.

Guests staying in one the suites get one VIP Fastpass per person valid for all their stay. This allows unlimited entry into all Fastpass attractions.

Guests staying in the Golden Forest Club Rooms get one Hotel Fastpass per day, allowing immediate entry to the Fastpass queue line to one attraction, except between 1:00pm and 4:00pm.

DINING:

Hunter's Grill – Buffet menu priced at €35 without drinks for an adult, and €19 with one drink for children.
Beaver Creek Tavern – Buffet menu priced at €35 without drinks for an adult, and €19 with one drink for children.
Redwood Bar and Lounge – Hotel Bar and Lounge.

Disney's Hotel Cheyenne

Themed to America's Old Wild West, with details from the Toy Story films, this 1000 room hotel is a 20-minute walk from the parks. A shuttle is also available.

The Cheyenne, along with the Santa Fe, are the resort's budget hotels and provide the best value for money. The rooms and services on offer are more basic than the other hotels, but you still have access to Extra Magic Hours, and you can still walk to the parks (or get a complimentary shuttle).

In terms of overall theming, we feel that this is one of the most well themed hotels with the buildings shaped to look like they are part of the Wild West.

Hotel rooms are being refurbished until September 2017. During renovation work, all the hotel amenities will be available at usual.

Room size: Standard rooms measure 21m^2.

Breakfast: Extra charge. £12 per day per adult and £11 per child if pre-booked.

Room Prices: 1 night is priced at €197 to €315, 2 nights is €282 to €519, 3 nights is €372 to €727. Additional nights are priced at €50 to €168.

Activities: Video games room; outdoor and indoor kids play areas; seasonal pony rides are available for an added charge. There is no pool at this hotel.

Extras: Free Wi-Fi is available at the bar and in the lobby only. Wi-Fi is not available in guest rooms at the time of writing but may be rolled out during the ongoing refurbishment.

DINING:

Chuck Wagon Café – Buffet. Continental breakfast (7:00am to 11:00am) is available. Lunch (12:30pm to 3:00pm) and dinner (6:00pm to 10:30pm) are buffets – €25.50 per adult without a drink, or €29 with one drink, and €16.50 per child. The adult buffet without a drink and the child buffet are included in the Hotel Meal Plan; the adult buffet with one drink is in Standard Meal Plan.

Red Garter Saloon – Hotel Bar, serving snacks and drinks.

Disney's Hotel Santa Fe

Themed to Santa Fe, in South West America, and with hints of Pixar's 'Cars' films. This 1000 room hotel is a 20-minute walk from the parks. A shuttle is also available.

The Santa Fe, along with Cheyenne, are the resort's budget hotels and provide the best value for money. The rooms and services on offer are more basic than the other hotels, but you still have access to Extra Magic Hours, and you can still walk to the parks (or get a shuttle).

In terms of theming, this is our least favourite hotel - the buildings do resemble those in real Santa Fe but it is not the most magical of themes.

This hotel is also marginally further away than the Cheyenne. It does, however, provide a relatively affordable option to stay on-site at a Disney hotel.

Room size: A standard room measures 21m² (up to 4 people plus 1 child under 3 years in a cot). Family rooms for up to 6 people are also available.

Breakfast: Extra charge. £12 per day per adult and £11 per child if pre-booked.

Room Prices: 1 night is priced at €197 to €315, 2 nights is €282 to €519, 3 nights is €372 to €727. Additional nights are priced at €50 to €168.

Activities: A video game arcade is available. There is no pool at this hotel.

Extras: Free Wi-Fi available is available throughout the hotel, including in guest rooms.

DINING:

La Cantina – Buffet from 6:00pm to 10:30pm. Continental breakfast is available. Buffet: €25.50 per adult without a drink, or €29 with a drink, and €16.50 per child. The adult buffet without a drink and the child buffet are included in Hotel Meal Plan; the adult buffet with one drink is included in Standard Meal Plan.

Rio Grande Bar – Hotel Bar. Serves snacks priced at €6-€7 and desserts priced at €4.

Disney's Davy Crockett Ranch

Unlike the other Disney properties, the Davy Crockett Ranch is not a hotel, but a 595-cabin campsite.

Davy Crockett Ranch is unlike any of the other accommodation covered in this section. It is not a standard hotel, but a campsite. Here you do not stay in a hotel room, but a large log cabin instead.

You truly do feel a world away from the theme parks in a serene environment. This accommodation is best for large groups with rooms for up to 6 people.

Davy Crockett Ranch is not located near any of the other on-site hotels, and is further than any of the partner hotels too. It is an 8km (15-minute) drive by car to the parks - you must provide your own transport as shuttle buses are not available.

Room size: There are both 1-bedroom (36m^2) and 2-bedroom (39m^2) cabins available. Cabins house up to 6 people. A Premium 2-bedroom cabin option is also available.

Breakfast: Extra charge. £8 per person per day if pre-booked.

Room prices: 1 night is priced at €216 to €284, 2 nights is €321 to €457, 3 nights is €430 to €634 for a standard bungalow. Additional nights are €69 to €137.

Activities: There is a stunning heated indoor swimming pool at this resort, as well as tennis courts, a video games arcade, pony rides, quad bikes, indoor and outdoor children's play areas, a small farm and an adventure ropes course (Davy's Crockett Adventure). Some activities require a surcharge.

Extras: Free Wi-Fi is available at the restaurant and the bar. In-room wired internet access is available at a surcharge. Daily cleaning of cabins is an extra charge. The Alamo Trading Post shop sells food, clothes and souvenirs.

DINING:

Davy Crockett's Tavern – Buffet. Buffet meals priced at €22 per adult and €10.50 per child.
Crockett's Saloon – Hotel Bar.

Partner Hotels

Partner hotels are located just outside the main Disneyland Paris resort land, but they are often much more affordable than Disney's own hotels.

❶ Radisson Blu Hotel

Number of rooms: 250 guest rooms and suites.
Room Size: Standard room (30m^2, maximum occupancy: 2 adults and 1 child aged under 3), Family room (30m^2, maximum occupancy: up to 4 adults), Junior Suite (60m^2), Suite (70m^2) and Presidential Suite (90m^2).
Breakfast: Included in most rates.
Room Prices: Sample price per person per night (based on 2 adults per room): €207.50
Activities: Swimming pool, fitness centre, spa, and outdoor play area. By the Disneyland Paris golf course, with 9 and 18-hole courses available to play on (extra charge).
Extras: Free Wi-Fi is throughout the hotel, including in rooms. Meeting rooms available.
Dining: Pamplemousse – French Table Service; Birdie – Buffet; and Le Chardon – Bar.

❷ Vienna International Dream Castle Hotel

Number of rooms: 397 rooms and suites.
Room Size: Double rooms and family rooms (28m^2), double queen rooms (44m^2), Rapunzel suite (54m^2), The Baron von Münchhausen Suite (60m^2) and The Royal Suite (220m^2).
Breakfast: Included in most rates.
Room Prices: Sample price per person per night (based on 2 adults per room): €154
Activities: Swimming pool, fitness centre, spa, indoor and outdoor play area, carousel, and a video game room.
Extras: Free Wi-Fi is available throughout the hotel, including in guest rooms.
Dining: Les Trois Mosquetaires – Buffet; and Excalibur – Bar.

❸ Vienna International Magic Circus Hotel

Number of rooms: 396 rooms and suites.
Room Size: Double rooms and family rooms (28m^2), and suites (up to 60m^2).
Breakfast: Included in most rates.
Room Prices: Sample price per person per night (based on 2 adults per room): €154
Activities: Swimming pool and fitness centre.
Extras: Free Wi-Fi is available throughout the hotel, including in guest rooms
Dining: L'Etoile – Buffet; and Bar des Artistes – Bar

MORE ABOUT PARTNER HOTELS

There is no Disney theming at these hotels but they are kid-friendly and staff have some knowledge of the theme parks. All these hotels provide frequent shuttle buses, and the longest shuttle bus ride is about 10 minutes. Wait times for buses may be up to 25 minutes in low seasons; buses are frequent (every 10 to 15 minutes) at peak times.

Most of the hotels also have a Disney shop where in-park purchases can be delivered. Partner hotels do not generally include city taxes when booked – these must be paid at check-in and are about €1 per adult per night. Book via a hotel aggregator such as Hotels.com or via Disneyland Paris' booking centre or website.

4 Adagio ApartHotel Marne la Valle - Val d'Europe
Number of rooms: 290 studios and apartments.
Room Size: Studios ($21m^2$), 1 to 3 bedroom apartments ($27m^2$ to $53m^2$)
Breakfast: Included in most rates in the breakfast room.
Room Prices: Sample price per person per night (based on 2 adults per room): €154
Activities: Swimming pool
Extras: Free Wi-Fi throughout the hotel, including in rooms. There is no restaurant (except for the buffet breakfast). Rooms include a kitchenette to cook your own meals.

5 Alongquin's Explorers Hotel
Number of rooms: 390.
Room Size: Standard crew rooms measure $18m^2$ to $22m^2$.
Breakfast: Included in most rates.
Room Prices: Sample price per person per night (based on 2 adults per room): €142
Activities: Swimming pool, play areas, video games room, and kids fitness area.
Extras: Free Wi-Fi is available throughout the hotel, including in guest rooms. Themed suites are also available including Planet Hollywood, Sweet and Jungle themes.
Dining: La Plantation – Buffet; Captain's Library – Table Service; Marco's Pizza – Quick Service; and The Traders – Bar

6 Hotel L'Elysée - Val d'Europe
Number of rooms: 152 rooms, including 4 executive suites.
Room Size: Cosy rooms ($24m^2$ - 2 person limit), family rooms ($24m^2$ - 4 person limit), family XL rooms (up to $48m^2$s - 8 person limit) and exec suites ($38m^2$ - 4 person limit).
Breakfast: Included in most rates.
Room Prices: Sample price per person per night (based on 2 adults per room): €139
Activities: No extra amenities.
Extras: Free Wi-Fi is available throughout the hotel, including in guest rooms. Meeting rooms are available. Laundry can be done for an additional charge.
Dining: Restaurant – Table service (lunch only); and L'Etoile – Bar.

7 Kyriad Hotel
Number of rooms: 300
Room Size: Standard rooms measure $18.5m^2$ for up to 4 people.
Breakfast: Included in most rates.
Room Prices: Sample price per person per night (based on 2 adults per room): €122.50
Activities: Carousel, video games room, and indoor children's play area.
Extras: Free Wi-Fi is available throughout the hotel, including in guest rooms.
Dining: Le Marché Gourmand – Buffet; and L'Abreuvoir – Bar

Tickets

There are many ways of buying park entry tickets for Disneyland Paris. Prices, special offers and ticket lengths vary depending on where you get your tickets from. To help you choose the best option for you, here is a detailed look at Disneyland Paris' tickets.

Important: If you have booked a Disney hotel through the Disneyland Paris website or over the phone, you can skip this section, as your tickets are included in your package unless you specifically asked for them not to be.

At the Park

Guests who turn up at Disneyland Paris spontaneously can buy tickets at the booths at the entrance of each theme park. As at the park you are a captive market, 'gate prices' (purchased on-site at Disneyland Paris) are the most expensive and you can get a substantial discount by booking in advance, and save *a lot* of time.

You can purchase one-park or two-park tickets for one or multiple days at any of the ticket booths. As well as the manned ticket booths, there are also automated ticket booths under the Disneyland Hotel.

Disney Stores

You can buy tickets at any Disney Store in the UK for Disneyland Paris and most Disney Stores around Europe. Tickets for Disneyland Paris may also be stocked at selected other Disney Stores worldwide. Just ask at the counter. These tickets are priced at theme park ticket booth rates, but will save you time queuing when at the resort as you can proceed directly to the turnstiles. If you are buying in advance, then we recommend you do so online to get the biggest savings.

GATE TICKET PRICES

1 day/1 park
Adults: €75; Children €67

1 day/2 parks
Adults: €90; Children €82

2 days/2 parks
Adults: €139; Children €126

3 days/2 parks
Adults: €174; Children €158

4 days/2 parks
Adults: €209; Children €190

5 days/2 parks
Adults: €229; Children €211.

Children are classed as 3 to 11 year olds. Children under 3 enter for free – proof of age may be requested.

Gate ticket prices last increased in March 2016.

The ticket booths for Disneyland Park are located under the pink Disneyland Hotel. Ticket booths for the Walt Disney Studios Park are located to the right of the entrance turnstiles of the park.

Online

If you purchase your tickets in advance online, you can make significant savings on the standard prices. The price varies depending on the date of your visit and visit length.

1-Day Tickets:
Billet Mini
- 1 Park – Adult: £36/€47; Child: £30/€40
- 2 Parks – Adult: £47/€62; Child: £42/€55

Billet Magic
- 1 Park – Adult: £45/€59; Child: £39/€52
- 2 Parks – Adult: £56/€74; Child: £51/€67

Super Magic Ticket
- 1 Park – Adult: £52/€69; Child: £47/€62
- 2 Parks – Adult: £64/€84; Child: £58/€77

Magic Flex Ticket
- 1 Park – Adult: £57/€75; Child: £51/€67
- 2 Parks – Adult: £68/€90; Child: £62/€82

Multi-Day Tickets:
- **2 days/2 parks**
Adult: £115/€139; Child: £104/€126

- **3 days/2 parks**
Adult: £144/€174; Child: £131/€158

- **4 days/2 parks**
Adult: £173/€209; Child: £157/€190

There are often two ticket offers available online: Pay for 3 days and get an extra day free, and pay for 4 days and get an extra day free.

Calendar: validity periods (valid vor tickets purchased from November the 3rd, 2016)

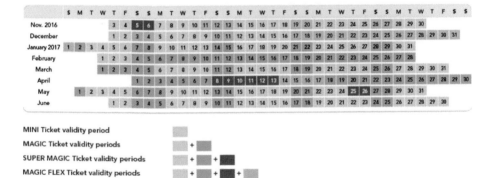

MINI Ticket validity period

MAGIC Ticket validity periods

SUPER MAGIC Ticket validity periods

MAGIC FLEX Ticket validity periods

MAGIC FLEX ticket 1 Day, valide for 1 year from the following day of purchase, without exclusions dates!

At the time of writing it is not possible to see which tickets are valid on which dates further than June 2017. The Disneyland Paris website will update throughout the year.

One-day tickets bought online can be purchased up to one day prior to the date of your visit. They cannot be used on the day of purchase itself.

If you opt to have the tickets posted to your home address (additional charges apply), the tickets must be purchased at least 10 days prior to the date of your visit.

TICKET BROKERS

There are also online ticket brokers that provide genuine discounted attraction tickets, sometimes with big savings! We recommend looking at: Attraction Tickets Direct, AttractionTix and 365Tickets.

Annual Passes

A Disneyland Paris Annual Pass gives you a year of benefits for the price of a few days' entry. Passes are available to all visitors. Pricing is valid until the end of November 2017.

Discovery - €139	Magic Flex - €189	Magic Plus - €249	Infinity - €399
Access to the parks 150 days per year. Cannot be used 2nd and 3rd day after activation.	Access to the parks 300 days per year.	Access to the parks 350 days per year.	Access to the parks 365 days per year.
Unlimited parking add-on for €40.	Unlimited parking is included.	Unlimited parking is included.	Unlimited preferred parking is included.
	Shops: 10% discount	Shops: 10% discount	Shops: 20% discount
	No dining discount	Dining: 10% discount	Dining: 15% discount
	Discount on Disney hotel room bookings.	Discount on Disney hotel room bookings.	Discount on Disney hotel room bookings.
	20% off 1-day park entry tickets for family/friends	20% off 1-day park entry tickets for family/friends	20% off 1-day park entry tickets for family/friends
	1-Year PhotoPass+ add-on for €55	1-Year PhotoPass+ add-on for €49	1-Year PhotoPass+ package included
		20% off Buffalo Bills Wild West Dinner Show	20% off Buffalo Bills Wild West Dinner Show
		10% off Golf Disneyland and at French Disney Stores	10% off Golf Disneyland and at French Disney Stores
		Ten 1 day/2 park tickets each year for only €39 each.	Twenty 1 day/2 park tickets each year for only €35 each.
		Dedicated park entrances, access to Extra Magic Hours, free locker, pushchair, kennel and wheelchair rentals & free non-alcoholic cocktail at Table Service Restaurants	Dedicated park entrances, access to Extra Magic Hours, free locker, pushchair, kennel and wheelchair rentals and free non-alcoholic cocktail at Table Service Restaurants
			VIP viewing locations for *Disney Illuminations* and *Disney Stars on Parade* - reserve in advance.
			Dedicated phone line with concierge service.
			Access to pools at certain Disney hotels.

Annual Pass Blockout Dates

Discovery Pass:
April 2017 - *Daily*
May 2017 - *1, 6, 7, 8, 13, 14, 20, 21, 25 to 28*
June 2017 - *3, 4, 5, 10, 11, 17, 18, 24, 25, 26*
July 2017 - *Daily*
August 2017 - Daily
September 2017 - *1, 2, 3, 9, 10, 16, 17, 23, 24 and 30*
October 2017 - *1, 7, 8, 14, 15, 21 to 31*
November 2017 - *1 to 5, 11, 12, 18, 19, 25 and 26*
December 2017 - *2, 3, 9, 10, 16, 17, 23 to 31*
January 2018 - *1 to 7*
February 2018 - *10 to 28*
March 2018 - 19, 20, 26 and 27
The Discovery pass cannot be used the two days following purchase.

Magic Flex Pass:
April 2017 - *8 to 17*
May 2017 - *1, 8, 25 and 26*
June 2017 - *3 to 5*
July 2017 - *None*
August 2017 - *None*
September 2017 - *None*
October 2017 - *7, 8, 14, 15, 21 to 31*
November 2017 - *1 to 5, 11 and 12*
December 2017 - *2, 3, 9, 10, 16, 17, 23 to 31*
January 2018 - *1 to 7*
February 2018 - *None*
March 2018 - *31*

Magic Plus Pass:
April 2017 - *None*
May 2017 - *None*
June 2017 - *None*
July 2017 - *None*
August 2017 - *None*
September 2017 - *None*
October 2017 - *27 to 31*
November 2017 - *1*
December 2017 - *26 to 31*
January 2018 - *None*
February 2018 - *None*
March 2018 - *None*

Blackout dates are days when your pass does not allow you entry into the parks. They do not apply on the day you buy your annual pass, but you cannot park-hop on the day you purchase an annual pass if it is a blackout date. There is a 20% family discount if buying five annual passes together.

How do I get my annual pass?

At the ticket booths ask whether they can do an annual pass there and then - this is often available on quieter days of the week, and some weekends. Alternatively, ask if "Donald's Desk" is open. If so, follow the directions and complete the passport there.

If the desk is not open you will buy a one-day ticket to go into Disneyland Park (not Walt Disney Studios Park). Once inside Disneyland Park, visit the "Bureau Pass Annuel" (located at the entrance of Discoveryland).

Here you will be asked for some details such as your address and name, have a photo taken for the card and have your annual pass made. The price of your day ticket will be deducted from your annual pass' price.

Allow about an hour for this, as there may be a queue of people – the actual process itself takes less than 10 minutes. Have a passport or ID card with you as proof of identity.

TICKET TIPS

1. 2-Park tickets are called "Hoppers" as they allow you to go from one park to the other park as many times as you wish on the same day.
2. If you are visiting for three days or longer, consider getting an Annual Passport. It provides discounts on food, hotels, merchandise and more.
3. Student tickets (ages 18 to 25 with proof) and Senior tickets (ages 60+ with proof) are available at the ticket booths. A "large family ticket" for families with at least 3 children is also available solely at the park entry ticket booths.

Disneyland Park

The first park at Disneyland Paris is composed of five lands filled with fantasy, adventure and excitement.

Disneyland Park, also known as *Parc Disneyland* in French, is based on the original Disneyland that opened in California in 1955. Every Disney resort around the world has one of these classic "Magic Kingdom-style" Disney parks. The park spans 140 acres, which is almost twice the size of the original.

Disneyland Park is the most visited theme park in Europe and the ninth most visited in the world, with 10.4 million visitors in 2015. The park has plenty to offer guests with almost fifty attractions (rides, themed areas and shows), as well as character experiences, dining options and plenty of places to shop.

Disneyland Park is, in our opinion, easily the best theme park in Europe, and it commonly heralded as the most beautiful Disney theme park in the world.

The park is divided into five areas (or "lands") around Sleeping Beauty Castle in the centre. These are Main Street USA, Frontierland, Adventureland, Fantasyland and Discoveryland. Each land has its own overarching theme, with its own soundtrack, décor, costumes and themed attractions. Around the edges of the park, you will find the Disneyland Railroad, which transports guests between these different lands.

We will now take a look at each land individually, as well as their attractions, dining options and other notable features.

As queuing is inevitable at theme parks, in order to help you determine how long you may wait to experience the attractions, we have included "average wait times"; these are for peak times such as school holidays (Summer, Christmas, Easter) and weekends throughout the year. Wait times outside busy times are often lower.

ATTRACTION KEY:
In the sections that follow, the following symbols are used when describing attractions.

 Fastpass?　　 On-Ride Photo?　　Average Wait Time

 Minimum Height　　Ride Length

Main Street, U.S.A.

Main Street, U.S.A. is the entrance to Disneyland Park, taking you towards Sleeping Beauty Castle and beyond.

Main Street, U.S.A. is the entrance area of Disneyland Park, leading you towards Sleeping Beauty Castle. It is themed to look like 1920s America.

It contains many shops on both sides of the street, the king of which is the **Emporium** where you are sure to find something to buy!

There are places to eat up and down the street too, including Quick Service and Table Service restaurants, as well as snack locations. There are also other food shops and carts around Main Street too.

Before entering Main Street, U.S.A. itself, there is Town Square with a gazebo in the centre.

City Hall is immediately to your left on Town Square; this is "Guest Services". Any questions you have can be answered here. They can also make reservations for tours and restaurants, and accept complaints and positive feedback too.

For disabled guests, an accessibility card is available at City Hall providing easier access to attractions. See our 'Guests with Disabilities' chapter for more information on this.

Running parallel to Main Street, U.S.A. are the **Liberty Arcade** and **Discovery Arcade**. These provide an alternative route for when it is raining.

Disney Imagineers learnt a valuable lesson from the other Disney theme parks, where Main Street, U.S.A. became congested during parades, shows and at the end of the day. The arcades allow an alternative route to Main Street, U.S.A. making the guest experience better.

You will often find character meet and greets in this area of the park, as well as live music.

Top Tip: As you walk up Main Street, U.S.A. listen to the sounds from the windows on the first floor to hear the noise that the residents of the town make. You can hear a dentist in one window, a man taking a bath in another and even a piano recital!

Attractions

Disneyland Railroad – Main Street Station

Take a grand tour of Disneyland Park on-board an authentic steam train. Whether you use it as a form of transportation, or just a way of seeing the sights, the Disneyland Railroad is a fun way to enjoy the park.

A full trip round the park takes 20 to 30 minutes.

This attraction usually ceases operation several hours before the park closes.

Main Street Vehicles and Horse-Drawn Streetcars

What better way to see Main Street, U.S.A. than from a vehicle – whether it is a horse-drawn car, a double decker bus or one of the other forms of transport.

These vehicles typically only operate in the morning.

Throughout the day, at unannounced times, the fountains in the moat of Sleeping Beauty Castle come to life, along with music, for special two to three minute happenings.

This takes place eight times per day but no schedule is officially published. If you are there on the hour or at half past the hour, you are more likely to see these.

These fountain shows change according to the seasons, with seasonal variations during Halloween, Christmas and St. Patrick's Day, for example.

DINING

Walt's Restaurant – Table Service. There are three different set menus priced from €40 to €70. The children's set menu is priced at €35. Some menu items are included in the Premium Meal Plan.

Casey's Corner – Counter Service. Serves ballgame themed snacks. Classic hot dogs - €7.50; 8-piece chicken nuggets - €8; salad - €7; desserts - €3 to €4; hot and cold drinks - €3.20 to €3.50; teatime treat - €5.60; beer - €5.40). Cheddar and onions can be added for a few cents more to the hot dogs.

Plaza Gardens – Buffet. Adult buffet priced at €35 with drinks. Child buffet priced at €18 with one drink. Both adult and child buffets with drinks are included in the Standard Meal Plan.

Victoria's Home-Style Restaurant – Counter Service. Hot sandwiches - €7; side salad - €3.50; crisps - €2.30; desserts - €3 to €4; hot and cold drinks €2.80 to €3.50; teatime treat - €5.60; beer - €5.40.

Frontierland

Step into Frontierland and be transported to the Wild West of the United States, and the town of Thunder Mesa.

Attractions

In addition to the attractions featured on the following pages, you may also wish to visit **Rustler Roundup Shootin' Gallery** where you can practice your shooting skills in a carnival-style game. There is an additional charge for this attraction.

Other attractions in this land include the **Frontierland Railroad Station**, the **Keelboats** which have been closed for several years, and **Pocahontas Indian Village** - a themed outdoor playground.

Big Thunder Mountain

Yes   1.02m   Yes   4 minutes   90 to 120 minutes

According to Disney legend, Big Thunder Mountain and the town of Thunder Mesa were discovered in the late 1800s.

In the town, a train line was constructed to transport ore around the mountain. However, the town was cursed and it was subsequently struck by an earthquake.

Residents left the town but a few years later the trains were found driving themselves around the mountain.

Guests can now take a 4-minute ride in one of these mine trains for themselves.

Along the way you will see collapsing bridges, experience a dynamite blast, see bats and feel much more on this wild ride!

Most of the action takes place on an island in the middle of the lake, making it a totally unique version of the ride when compared to other Disney parks.

It is also the longest, tallest and fastest of the Big Thunder Mountain rides around the world but is by far the most family-friendly of the resort's roller coasters.

At the end, you can also purchase your on-ride photo if you wish.

This is definitely one of our favourite attractions in the park and should not be missed.

The ride came out of a year-long update in December 2016 and is more explosive than ever before!

Phantom Manor

🎟 No | 🎢 None | 📷 No | ✓ 7 minutes | ⌛ Less than 30 minutes

Venture through this derelict manor as you discover the story of Melanie, a bride.

On her wedding day, Melanie eagerly awaited her groom, not knowing that a phantom haunted the house she was in. The phantom lured the groom into the attic and hung him. Melanie waited for her groom but he never turned up. Now, she roams around the manor still in her wedding dress.

Phantom Manor is definitely a must-see attraction: the atmosphere, music and details are amongst the best in the whole resort.

The storyline of this attraction is completely unique, despite similar rides existing at other Disney parks worldwide.

The audio in the initial walk-through section of the attraction is only in French, which can make the attraction more difficult to understand for international visitors, but this is just a short part of the whole experience and a prelude to the ride itself.

After the walk-through pre-show, guests sit in "doombuggies" for the ride portion of the attraction. These rotate and tilt to show guests parts of the mansion as they venture through it.

You can expect to see pianos playing by themselves, door knockers that have a mind of their own, and ghosts gathering for a ballroom dance.

Throughout the attraction, there are no jump-out scares but the initial walk-through section may frighten some children due to the effects used here, and the dark. The animatronics in the 'cemetery' scene may also frighten young children. These pass by relatively quickly.

Phantom Manor is in no way a horror-maze attraction, and as there is no height restriction, the attraction is accessible to all ages. However, do be wary of younger kids.

If you are unsure whether your child will be comfortable with the ride, try doing it in the daytime when the building is least imposing.

Also, try not to make this your first ride as there are countless stories of children doing Phantom Manor at the start of a trip and then refusing to do any other rides as they are scared.

If you are really unsure as to the ride's suitability, try watching an on-ride video online before your visit.

We highly recommend making a stop at this ride as it is a true Disney classic, and as Melanie says: "Be sure to bring your death certificate. We're just *dying* to have you."

Thunder Mesa Riverboat Landing

No	None	No	15 minutes	Less than 30 minutes

Set sail on a classic riverboat around Big Thunder Mountain and admire Frontierland's stunning landscape.

The Thunder Mesa Riverboat is a relaxing change from the crowds of the park with space to roam around the boat.

There are some (limited) seating areas and you can hear the story of the Molly Brown riverboat as you go around the river via the speakers, though the audio is not particularly loud - most people are just take in the atmosphere.

Top Tip: The Riverboat's operating hours are shorter than most other attractions in the park. It usually opens one hour after park opening, and ceases operation in the middle of the afternoon or early evening.

THERE'S MORE TO FRONTIERLAND THAN MEETS THE EYE

In addition to the major attractions featured on these pages, you should also be sure to enjoy the little details that make Frontierland a unique land. As you walk into Frontierland from Central Plaza, be sure to stop by **Fort Comstock**, this is the timber-themed entrance to the land. Notice all the little details in this area and if the steps are open on your left, be sure to climb up and get a different perspective on this land.

Phantom Manor has its own cemetery at the exit called **Boot Hill** that many guests miss. When you come out of the attraction, you can either turn right down the hill towards the front of the manor, or you can continue straight ahead to Boot Hill. This area contains tombstones of a number of Thunder Mesa residents. All of the tombstones tell their own story through the use of gags and rhymes. You can also access Boot Hill if you are not riding Phantom Manor by making your way up the hill to the right of the house.

Even the restaurants and shops are filled with details. Inside, **The Lucky Nugget Saloon** there is a stage, where live music and others acts occasionally perform. **Cowboy Cookout BBQ** also has live music, and the Imagineers went to town with the theming here. Notice the chairs, for example - unlike other restaurants where everything is uniform, here there are dozens of different chairs of all types and styles because in the Wild West the townsfolk would bring their own chairs from home.

Chaparral Theater

| No | None | No | 20 minutes | Until next show |

The Chaparral Theater is Frontierland's stage, and holds regular shows. The theatre is outdoors with a covered roof, meaning it can get chilly in the winter, but it is sheltered from the rain. Usually one of the following two shows is playing here.

Top Tip: Be sure to sit in a seat towards the centre, as the theatre has been badly designed with two big ceiling supports in front of the stage. These supports can block your view if you do not plan accordingly.

The Forest of Enchantment

This is a Disney musical spectacular, with live singing and shows in English and French. You can expect to see your favourite characters and hear songs from Tangled, The Jungle Book, Pocahontas, Tarzan and more. Many original characters are also present.

This truly is a fantastic show and is not to be missed.

Frozen Sing-Along

Join Anna, Elsa and Olaf, who appear live on stage performing well-known songs from the hit film 'Frozen'. The audience are encouraged to join in by singing along to lyrics shown on screens.

'Frozen Sing-Along' is presented in separate English and French shows – refer to the Times Guide for their schedules. This show is very popular and you usually will need to queue up at least 30 minutes before the show you want to see begins.

DINING

Silver Spur Steakhouse – Table Service. The 2-course Sheriff menu is €30, and the 3-course Sheriff menu is €37 - both without drinks. A 3-course Cowboy menu is €43. Main courses are €22 to €40 a la carte. The children's menu is €18 with one drink and €33 for the premium menu. The children's set menu and 3-course Sheriff menu are on the Plus Meal Plan. The kid's Premium Menu is on the Premium Meal Plan.

The Lucky Nugget Saloon – Counter Service. Set menus are priced at €22 for an adult, and €12 for a child.

Cowboy Cookout Barbecue – Counter Service. Set menus are priced at €12 to €16 for adults and €8.50 for children.

Fuente del Oro – Counter Service serving Mexican fare. Set menus are priced at €12 to €15. The children's menu is priced at €8.50.

Last Chance Cafe – Counter Service. Take-away snack meals are €7 to €11. Desserts, beer, and hot and cold drinks are also available.

Adventureland

Venture into an Arabian story, the Caribbean or a temple with Indiana Jones.

Attractions

In addition to the attractions covered below, you may also want to check out **Adventure Isle** (a walk through area with winding paths, caves, a pirate ship and a suspension bridge), **Le Passage Enchante d'Aladdin** (a walkthrough attraction depicting scenes from the story of Aladdin) and **La Plage des Pirates** (an outdoor playground).

Indiana Jones et le Temple du Peril:

| | Yes | 1.40m | No | 2 minutes | 30 to 60 minutes |

This roller coaster ride will take you on an archaeological adventure through the lost Temple of Doom.

Your adventure will have you climbing in search of treasure, dropping, going around tight corners and meandering in and around the Temple, even descending rapidly into a 360-degree loop as your mine cart goes out of control.

The ride has the biggest minimum-height limit of any ride at any Disney park worldwide – 140cm. It was also the first Disney roller coaster in the world to go upside down. The ride even ran backwards for a few years, but now runs forward once again.

This is one of the most intense coasters at the resort with the loop being particularly tight. It is also quite a rough ride.

Of all the coasters in the park, it usually has the shortest queue as it is hidden at the back of the park, and the big minimum height means it is off-limits to most kids under the age of 10.

Overall, it is relatively short but a fun experience.

Top Tip: When park attendance is low, Fastpass is not offered at this attraction.

Top Tip 2: Although this attraction can get long wait times, it is almost always deserted after the daily parade.

Pirates of the Caribbean

No | None | Yes | 10 minutes | 15 to 45 minutes

Ahoy me hearties! Set sail through the world of the Pirates of the Caribbean at Disneyland Paris.

Board a boat and enjoy a ten-minute journey into a fort invaded by pirates.

Your boat will ascend and go down two short flume drops. You are unlikely to get wet, but it may happen.

The audio-animatronic characters in the attraction are enthralling, and it may just be the best themed attraction in all of Disneyland Park. The attention to detail is fantastic, from the queue line to the Cast Members' costumes and the music to the sets.

This attraction is based on the original Pirates of the Caribbean ride in Disneyland in California. Pirates of the Caribbean was the final ride Walt Disney himself supervised the creation of at Disneyland.

Be aware that the queue line for the ride is not well lit due to the atmosphere it aims to create, and therefore it is very dark. This will especially strike you during the daytime when your eyes take a while to adjust, so we would advise holding onto your children's hands throughout the queue line.

This ride's loading system is very efficient and it has the highest capacity in the park, but it is also an extremely popular ride. This means that although most of the year waits stay below 20 minutes, on peak days you may see these rise to 60 minutes. The queue line is almost constantly moving and once you are in the indoor section there is a lot to see.

The recommended minimum age for this attraction is one year old as it is very dark and loud.

This a must-see, family-friendly ride that is a classic Disney experience.

Important: This version of the attraction is currently the only version of the ride not to feature the characters from the famous "Pirates of the Caribbean" blockbusters. However, the ride will be undergoing a large refurbishment from January 2017 to summer 2017 when the famous pirate is expected be added into the ride. During this refurbishment, the ride will be closed to guests.

Warning: As the queue line for this attraction is so dark and there are so many people in one place, it is a notorious favourite spot for pickpockets – especially when there are long waits. Be aware of your surroundings.

La Cabane des Robinson

No	None	No	5 minutes	None - walkthrough

Enter the world of Swiss Family Robinson as you explore the treehouse built from the wood of their shipwreck. You can see the complex water wheel system they built to get water up to the bedrooms, and explore the kitchen, living rooms and bedrooms. This is a walkthrough experience and kids generally enjoy exploring, and climbing the steps.

From the top, the view is mostly obscured by leaves but you can get an interesting perspective on the park from up here.

ADVENTURELAND IS DESIGNED TO BE EXPLORED ON FOOT...

Of all the lands at Disneyland Park, Adventureland is the one that appears to have the smallest number of attractions. However, this area of the park is filled with incredible details that you need to find for yourself outside of the main attractions. Adventureland is built around Adventure Isle, with La Cabane des Robinson at the centre. As well as the treehouse, be sure to step aboard the **Pirate Galleon** moored in the centre of the land, and explore the caves under the treehouse to see the secrets that lie here. There are also a separate set of **caves** next to the galleon - here you will find treasure, skeletons and cascading waterfalls. Be sure to follow the signs to "Pont Suspendu" to reach **Spyglass Hill** and enjoy the stunning view over the park. Don't forget to cross the wobbly **Suspension Bridge**, and the **Floating Bridge** ("Pont Flotant") which is located next to the Swiss Family Robinson's shipwreck.

DINING

Blue Lagoon – Table Service. Adult set menus are priced between €32 and €55. The children's set menu is priced at €18, with a premium kids' menu priced at €31.50. Select menus and items are on the Plus and Premium Meal Plans.

Agrabah Cafe – Buffet. The adult buffet is €33 with one drink. The children's buffet is €18 with one drink. Both the child buffet, and the adult buffet are included in the Standard Meal Plan.

Colonel Hathi's Pizza Outpost – Counter Service. Set menus are priced between €12 and €15. The children's set menu is priced at €8.50.

Hakuna Matata – Counter Service. Set menus are priced at €12 to €15. The children's set menu is priced at €8.

Coolpost – Snacks. Hot dogs - €7.50; teatime drink and donut - €5.60; ice creams - €3 to €4; and crepes - €3 to €4. Other small snacks, as well as hot and cold drinks are sold.

Fantasyland

Find classic Disney attractions here, in this land dedicated to the youngest members of your family.

Attractions

Disneyland Park's gentle toddler-friendly rides are here in the most magical of all the lands, and there is plenty of variety. In addition to the attractions covered in depth on the following pages, you may also want to visit **Sleeping Beauty Castle** that houses **The Dragon's Lair** *(La Tanière du Dragon)* and **Sleeping Beauty's Gallery** *(La Galerie de la Belle au Bois Dormant)*. These are both great detailed walk-through attractions. The Dragon's Lair contains a huge animatronic dragon that may be frightening for children.

Top Tip: Fantasyland closes one hour before the rest of the park each day in order to clear the area for the nightly fireworks show.

Peter Pan's Flight

FP Yes	None	No	4 minutes	60 to 90 minutes

Peter Pan's Flight is one of Disneyland Paris' most popular rides. It features beloved characters, it is family-friendly and provides a small thrill too.

Hop aboard a flying pirate ship and take a voyage through the world of Peter Pan and Never Never Land.

As you soar, you will see scenes to the sides and underneath you, in a retelling of the classic story.

The ride's interior is stunning from the moment you step in, and truly immersive.

This is an incredibly popular ride, so using a Fastpass is recommended to avoid a long wait.

Alternatively, visit the attraction early in the morning, in the evening before Fantasyland closes, or during the parade. On busy days, Fastpasses will run out by midday.

Important: Visitors who are afraid of heights may find this ride unsuitable. The flying ships you sit in really do give the sensation of flight and at times you will be several metres off the ground and descending steeply (albeit not too quickly). These sensations may surprise some guests – mostly, though, it seems to be adults who are affected by this, and not children.

Alice's Curious Labyrinth

🎟 No	📏 None	📷 No	🕐 10 minutes	⏳ None - Walkthrough

Ever fancied getting lost in the world of Alice in Wonderland? Well now you can do exactly that!

This maze has a good variation of elements and is just challenging enough to keep you guessing where to go next. There are quite a few fun photos to take along the way too.

Once you reach the end of the maze, you have the option of returning back to the park, or climbing the Queen's Castle first. The climb is worth doing for the stunning view over the park. The labyrinth is good family fun and a good way for the little ones to burn some energy.

Lancelot's Carousel

⏳ Under 20 minutes	🎟 No	🕐 2 minutes	📏 None

This is a beautiful, vintage lined with golden horses, and is a joy to ride for every member of the family.

Whether you want to go along with the theme of Lancelot's carousel or prefer to think of it as the carousel from Mary Poppins, it is sure to be a fun-filled family adventure.

Meet Mickey Mouse

🎟 No	📏 None	📷 Yes	🕐 1 to 2 minutes	⏳ 60 to 90 minutes

Mickey is preparing backstage for his next magic show and you have the chance to meet him. The queue line features short films playing on a big screen to ease the wait.

Once you reach the front of the queue, you will be taken to a room with Mickey inside. Here you can meet the big cheese, have a chat, and get an autograph and photos.

You are welcome to take your own photos and/ or ask the Cast Member present to help you. In addition, there is a Disney photographer there who will also take an official photo, which can be purchased at the attraction's exit.

"it's a small world"

FUN FACT

This ride has more audio-animatronics that any other attraction in at Disneyland Paris.

	No		None		No		10 minutes		Less than 20 minutes

'It's a small world' is one of the resort's most memorable and popular attractions, featuring hundreds of dolls singing a song about the uniting of the world. You can guarantee you will remember the lyrics.

Guests board a boat and travel leisurely through scenes depicting countries from around the world, as the attraction's song plays in various languages.

The loading system is incredibly efficient on this ride, meaning that the number of people who can enjoy the ride every hour is high – for you, this means that queues are often very short.

This ride is a great Disney classic that, although not based on any film franchise, is one of the "must-dos" for many visitors.

Blanche Neige et les Sept Nains

	No		None		No		2 minutes		20 to 40 minutes

Relive the tale of Snow White for yourself in this classic ride filled with light-hearted scenes, as well as many darker scenes too.

In the U.S.A., this same ride is called "Snow White's Scary Adventures", which gives you a bit of an idea of the scare level of the ride. The Evil Witch in particular makes surprise appearances out of every corner, the dark woods have ominous trees, and loud thunder and lightning effects may startle younger children.

Although the ride itself is slow moving, the loud noises and the character of the Evil Witch are likely to scare young children.

Mad Hatter's Teacups

	Under 30 minutes		No
	2 minutes		None

Hop inside a teacup and go for a wild spin with the Mad Hatter.

The ride functions much like any other teacup ride around the world, where you have a wheel at the centre of the cup that you can turn to spin yourself round faster. Or, leave it alone and have a more relaxing spin.

Sleeping Beauty Castle
Le Château de la Belle au Bois Dormant

Standing 51m (167ft) tall, *Le Château de la Belle au Bois Dormant*, is the centrepiece and icon of Disneyland Park.

Unlike the castles in the American Disney theme parks, when the Imagineers were designing Disneyland Park, they knew that the castle here had to be different. The European audience were used to seeing real castles, and therefore the park's icon version had to be more fairytale-inspired than real.

The attention to detail is stunning, even including little snails (or *escargots*) on the turrets at the top, and the trees in front of the castle are cut into a square shape just like in the 1959 'Sleeping Beauty' film.

The castle is not just for show, however, and can actually be explored by guests. On the ground floor you can walk along the drawbridge and over the moat to enjoy this magical building from the inside.

To the right hand side of the castle, you can see a small wishing well where characters occasionally meet.

Behind the castle, you can find the **Sword in the Stone**. Try to remove it if you can, and be crowned king or queen of the kingdom.

Inside the castle, you can enjoy two unique shops, which are incredibly well-themed: enjoy Merlin the Magician's shop on the left, and a year-round Christmas shop on the right.

Once you are done with your shopping, take the winding staircase up the first floor and see the story of Sleeping Beauty retold using tapestries and beautiful **stained-glass windows**. You can even step foot onto the balcony outside for a stunning view over Fantasyland.

The Castle's biggest secret, however, is altogether more hidden. When looking at the castle from the front, instead of taking the drawbridge, take the path on the left instead. This will lead you through a dark passageway into **The Dragon's Lair**.

Here lies an enormous animatronic dragon (at the time, the biggest in the world) in an area unlike any other Disney theme park around the world. Every few minutes the dragon may just come to life. You can also access the lair through Merlin's shop.

Dumbo - The Flying Elephant

No	None	No	90 seconds	60 to 90 minutes

Dumbo is one of the most popular rides in the whole of Disneyland Paris across the two parks.

Situated right in the centre of Fantasyland, it offers views of the surrounding area, as well as being a whole lot of fun.

In front of the seats in each flying elephant there is a lever that allows you to lift your Dumbo up or down and fly up to 7 metres (23ft) high!

As the ride is popular, slow loading, and has a low capacity, there are long waits all day from this attraction.

Ride it during the parade, during Extra Magic Hours, or at the start or end of the day for the shortest waits. It handles less than 1000 guests an hour; in comparison 'Pirates of the Caribbean' handles over three times as many guests in a single hour.

The Adventures of Pinocchio

No	None	No	2 minutes	20 to 45 minutes

Ride through a retelling of the story of Pinocchio and see the tales from the book come to life.

As with the film, there are also some darker moments that may frighten younger

children, though these do pass by quickly. It is much less frightening than Snow White's attraction, for example.

This ride is not a major attraction like Peter Pan's

Flight but it still draws in moderately sized queues due to the popularity of the characters.

Casey Jr: The Circus Train

No	None	No	2 minutes	20 to 45 minutes

Based on the character from Dumbo, Casey Junior is the little circus train that will take you on a ride around models of sets from classic Disney films.

This is a great ride for the whole family, and although it is not technically a roller coaster, it can be a good way of seeing whether the kids (or adults) are up to a slightly wilder ride, though this ride is still very tame compared to the other coasters at Disneyland Paris.

There is no height restriction, so everyone can ride this attraction, and the low speed is unlikely to frighten anyone.

You will whiz by castles and other story pieces from Disney's classic tales during your ride. For a more leisurely view of these scenes try the Storybook Canal Boats located next door.

Note that adults may feel a bit cramped on this ride - and two adults next to each other will have to squeeze in tightly!

Unfortunately, the ride is often closed or only opened for limited periods during the off-season. It also usually closes two to three hours before the rest of Fantasyland.

Princess Pavilion

No	None	No	2 minutes	60 to 90 minutes

The Princess Pavilion is your chance to meet one of the Disney princesses. Then chat, play, get an autograph and take some photos.

Outside the attraction, there is a sign that will inform you of which princesses you will meet at the end of the queue and at what time each princess is present.

If seeing a particular princesses is a priority, we suggest you visit the *Princess Pavilion* as early as possible, as queue lines build up quickly.

In the past, the Pavilion has also used a reservation system, whereby you go to a nearby machine, get a reservation time slot to return, and then queue to see the princesses. This system has not been in operation for a while, but may return at any time.

Le Pays des Contes de Fees - **Storybook Canal Boats**

| No | None | No | 2 minutes | Less than 20 minutes |

This is a nice, relaxing ride, where you set in boats and sail by models of classic childhood tales.

Along your serene journey, you will see scenes from the Little Mermaid, Hansel and Gretel, Fantasia, Snow White, the Wizard of Oz and many more.

You will even enter the famous cave from Aladdin, and see the Genie's lamp shining brightly.

It is a nice change of pace from some of the busier attractions in the park and you can take some great photos of the models.

This is a great attraction for very young children who can look around without anything potentially being scary.

If you want a different perspective on these same scenes, and a faster pace, consider riding Casey

Junior instead.

This attraction almost always has low wait times, as many people do not know this section of the park exists.

This attraction also usually closes two to three hours before the rest of Fantasyland, and may be closed during the off-season.

DINING

Auberge de Cendrillon – Table Service. This is a premium restaurant where all the Disney Princesses (and their accompanying princes) are present. They will perform dances throughout the meal, and visit every table to meet guests too. The adult set menu is priced at €75 and children's set menu is priced at €45. This meal can be pre-booked and pre-paid as part of a Disneyland Paris package.

Au Chalet de la Marionette – Counter Service. Set menus are priced between €12 and €15, children's set menus are priced at €9.

Pizzeria Bella Notte – Counter Service. Set menus are priced between €12 and €15, children's set menus are €8.50. Serves pizza, rigatoni pasta and lasagne.

Toad Hall Restaurant – Counter Service. Set menus are priced at €12 to €15, children's set menus are €8.50. Serves fish and chips, and chicken sandwiches.

The Old Mill – Snack location. Serves waffles (gaufres) with/without chocolate (€3.80 to €4), crisps at €2.30, cake at €4, ice creams at €3.50 to €4, and hot & cold drinks.

Fantasia Gelati – Snack location. Serves Italian-style scoop ice cream. €3 to €4 per ice cream, €3 for a hot drink.

Discoveryland

Take a look into the future… from the minds of the past. Discoveryland is inspired by retro-futuristic visions of space and beyond.

Attractions

Some of the park's most popular and thrilling attractions are located in this land. In addition to the attractions listed below, you can go on a trip around the park at the **Disneyland Railroad** Discoveryland Station.

Star Wars Hyperspace Mountain: Rebel Mission

FP	Yes		1.32m	📷	Yes	⌄	2 minutes	⧗	60 to 90 minutes

Important: As part of the park's Experience Enhancement refurbishment program, *Space Mountain* is closed from January 2017 to May 2017 to add new, more comfortable trains. It will re-open as *Hyperspace Mountain*, themed to Star Wars inside - we expect new lighting, projections, music and special effects. It is not clear if this will be a temporary of permanent change.

Hyperspace Mountain is a thrilling roller coaster through space, and it is our favourite coaster at the resort.

It is the only Space Mountain in the world to have inversions and loops, as well as a high-speed launch. It is also the grandest and roughest of all the Space Mountain rides around the world, and the beautiful steampunk-style building is the centrepiece for Discoveryland.

As you soar through space, you will come across comets, supernovas, meteorites and elements from the Star Wars saga, before landing back in Discoveryland. A must-do ride for thrill seekers!

Top Tip: This ride has a Single Rider queue line so if you are alone, or do not mind being separated from your party, you can use it drastically reduce your wait time.

Les Mystères de Nautilus

No   None   No   5 minutes   None - Walkthrough

Explore Captain Nemo's ship, the Nautilus, from "20,000 Leagues under the Sea".

This incredibly detailed walkthrough takes you under the sea and into the heart of the captain's submarine.

This attraction truly is a fantastic work of art and includes some special effects inside such as a giant squid attack, as well as an incredible level of theming and detail.

Kids are unlikely to be entertained, however, as it is a simple walkthrough.

Be aware that some of the effects like the engine room may startle younger members of the family. It is also a bit dark in certain sections inside, but manageable for most people.

Insider Secret: Although you may believe you are inside the Nautilus ship, the winding staircase you use to enter this attraction is designed to disorientate you. Instead of walking towards the ship, you are actually walking down a long corridor and into a show building located between Autopia and Discoveryland Theatre – the exact opposite direction from the Nautilus.

Discoveryland Theatre

Formerly home to Michael Jackson's 'Captain EO', the Discoveryland Theatre is now home to the "Disney & Pixar Short Film Festival".

Guests can put on their 3D glasses and enter the imaginative worlds of three animated shorts – Get A Horse, For The Birds and La Luna.

These showings are enhanced with motion and in-theatre effects when available.

This is not hugely mind-blowing as an attraction but it seems to be a temporary addition until it can be replaced in a few years' time. It is, nevertheless, a good way to relax for a short period of time, and watch a short film, whilst finding some much-needed air-con in the summer (and heating the winter).

Show lengths vary depending on what is being shown. You should never have to wait longer than until the next showing starts.

Star Tours: The Adventures Continue

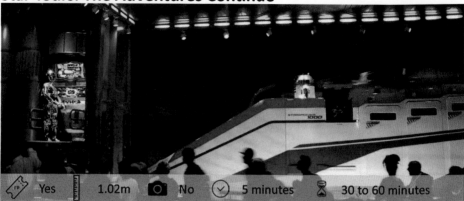

Yes | 1.02m | No | 5 minutes | 30 to 60 minutes

Star Wars fans will fall in love with *Star Tours*, but this attraction is equally fun for those who have never seen the films. This is a definite must-do.

Once in the queue line, you will enter an intergalactic spaceport, with adverts for various destinations and overhead announcements of flights leaving.

As you travel through the terminal you will see Star-Speeders (your transport vehicle), an alien air traffic control station, R2-D2, C3PO, and many robots hard at work to make your journey to space unforgettable.

You will then board your StarSpeeder vehicle for your trip to one of many planets from the Star Wars universe.

With over 50 different randomised scenes, you never know what planet you will explore on your next ride.

Almost the entirety of the dialogue is in French, but it is the visuals along with the movement that really matter here; the simulator does feel incredibly realistic and it is a great ride.

Be advised that if you are prone to motion sickness, or are scared of confined spaces, you should skip Star Tours.

Top Tip: If you want a milder ride, ask to be seated in the front row. This is the centre of the ride vehicle and therefore reduces the sensations felt. For a more thrilling experience, ask to be sat in the back row.

A brand new permanent Star Wars meet and greet location called "StarPort" is also available in front of Star Tours from March 2017.

Buzz Lightyear Laser Blast

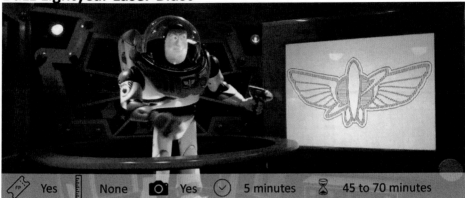

FP Yes	None	📷 Yes	⊙ 5 minutes	⧖ 45 to 70 minutes

On this interactive ride, once you have sat down in your Space Cruiser, you can use its laser guns to shoot at the targets around you – you will be helping out Buzz Lightyear and racking up points.

Different targets are worth different amounts of points and there are even

hidden targets so you can score thousands of bonus points.

At the end of the ride, the person with the most points wins. It is competitive, fun and endlessly re-rideable – it is also a great family adventure with no minimum height limit.

If you buy an attraction photo at the end, you can get your scores printed onto the photos too!

Top Tip: The highest scoring target is directly in front of Zurg – shoot his medallion repeatedly to get a huge number of points.

Orbitron: Machines Volantes

FP No	None	📷 No	⊙ 90 seconds	⧖ 30 to 60 minutes

Soar above Discoveryland in your very own spaceship.

This is a spinning-type ride similar to Dumbo in Fantasyland, but the ships

here go higher, spin faster and tilt more, making for a surprisingly good thrill.

It is a lot of fun but it is not a must-do attraction as it is far from being unique.

Note: It is a very tight fit for two adults in one spaceship, so avoid this. An adult and a child will fit in a spaceship fine, however.

Autopia

 No | See Below | No | ⊙ 5 minutes | ⧗ 60 to 90 minutes

Hop aboard one of these little cars and take it for a spin around Discoveryland.

Autopia is hugely popular with kids who get to drive a car for the very first time.

The cars are guided on rails so guests cannot really go too far wrong but the little ones (and bigger ones too) can steer and accelerate around the track and 'race' others.

The ride is great fun and is definitely worth a visit.

Riders under 0.81m may not ride. Riders between 0.81m and 1.32m must be accompanied by someone over the 1.32m height minimum. Riders over 1.32m may ride alone.

Videopolis Theatre – Jedi Training Academy

At *Jedi Training Academy*, young children can learn to harness *The Force* and become a Jedi. Once on-stage, the kids perform several moves with their lightsabers and even battle Darth Vader and some Storm Troopers.

Shows are performed in English and French at the same time – with the Cast Member repeating each sentence in both languages.

The show is entertaining even without having a kid of your own taking part. A proud parent will love it even more.

There is no need to turn up more than 20 minutes before show time if your child is not participating, as there are plenty of seats.

To be part of the show, participants must be aged between 7 and 12, and must report to Videopolis Theatre at the time stated in the in-park Times Guide.

There are only 16 spaces per show. Young padawans should return 45 minutes before the show starts for training.

Shows are about 15 minutes in length and you do not usually need to turn up more than 15 minutes in advance.

DINING

Buzz Lightyear's Pizza Planet – Buffet with unlimited soft drinks. €20 for adults, €12 for children. This restaurant may be permanently closed.

Cafe Hyperion – Counter Service. Adult set menus are priced at €12 to €15, and children's set menus priced are €8.50.

Fireworks

Disney theme parks around the world are renowned for ending visitors' days by lighting up the sky with incredible firework displays. Disneyland Paris is no exception.

Disney Illuminations is Disneyland Paris' dazzling nighttime spectacular which coordinates music, projections, lasers, water fountains and fireworks.

Of all the nighttime spectaculars we have seen at Disney theme parks across the world, *Disney Illuminations* is easily the most impressive.

You can expect to see scenes from Star Wars, Frozen, Pirates of the Caribbean, The Little Mermaid, The Lion King and Finding Nemo.

Disney Illuminations is performed nightly at the closing of Disneyland Park. The show runs for 22-minutes. After the fireworks, Main Street, U.S.A. remains open for about 45 minutes after the park closes for your shopping convenience.

In addition, there are other fireworks shows offered on select nights such as Bastille Day and New Year's Eve. On these days, the themed firework display is first, followed by *Illuminations*.

During the Christmas season, *Disney Illuminations* is replaced by an entirely different show, *Disney Dreams of Christmas*, which celebrates the most wonderful time of the year.

Walt Disney Studios Park does not offer a night-time show throughout the year, except on New Year's Eve.

Lake Disney, by the on-site hotels, offers fireworks on select dates around Bonfire Night and on New Year's Eve too. Admission is free to Lake Disney.

DISNEY ILLUMINATIONS TOP TIPS:

1: To get the best spot for *Disney Illuminations*, we recommend you be in place a minimum of 60 minutes before the show begins. Some people stake out spots over an hour in advance.

2: Find a spot with a railing in front of you – this prevents someone from turning up during the show and obscuring your view. This happens often with guests who put their children on their shoulders as the show begins, ruining the view for everyone behind them. Equally frustrating is someone filming the whole show on their phone.

3: After the show, only Main Street, U.S.A. remains open. There are three main toilet locations for you to use – the first, and the least crowded, is located by the Baby Care Center (Zone J on the map overleaf). The second is inside the arcades running alongside Main Street. The third is at the end of Main Street, U.S.A. and to the right of the Disneyland Railroad station at the Arboretum (Zone P).

Disney Illuminations Viewing Guide

Disney Illuminations is primarily a projections show that relies heavily on you having a view of the front of Sleeping Beauty Castle.

Although the fireworks can be seen from across the park, you will not understand the show's storyline if you are not viewing the front of the castle and its projections.

The front is also where the lasers, fountains and fire effects can be seen, as well as the Second Star to the Right on the castle.

You will want to position yourself at the central plaza (hub) area of the park or along Main Street, U.S.A. for the best view.

To help you decide on the best view of *Disney Illuminations*, we have created this helpful guide – note that the zones or areas in the diagram have been created by us and there are no delineations between the areas when you are in the park itself.

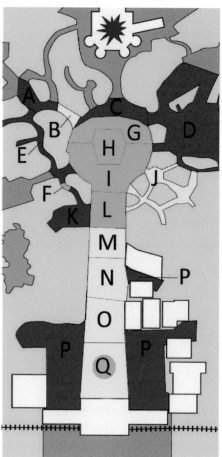

Zone A – A very off-centre view of the show. Uncrowded but not worth it.

Zone B – A better view than from Zone A. Uncrowded but an off-centre view. Good if you want to see the show last-minute from a decent angle. You may get wet here.

Zone C – Many guests sit or stand here but this zone is too close to Sleeping Beauty Castle for your enjoyment. You will miss some or all of the fireworks behind the castle. The projections will also not have their full effect as you will be too close, and you will also likely get very wet from the water fountains.

Zone D – This area is often cleared by Cast Members and may or may not be open to guests. Even when the area is open views are far from ideal.

Zone E – Views from this area are obstructed by trees, and provide no visibility.

Zone F – Located off-centre. Behind and to the left of the Disney Illuminations control booth. If you are positioned by the railing here, you will get a fantastic view of the show – this location can only accommodate a few people.

Zone G – This is where guests who arrive early will position themselves. This area provides a decent view of the show, and you will be able to see all fireworks and effects. It is however, still too close to the action for you to appreciate the show fully, in our opinion. Part of the area on the left of Zone G will be reserved for people with disability cards and people accompanying them.

Zone H – Faces Sleeping Beauty Castle head-on and is far back enough to provide a good view of the whole show. It is not the perfect view but it is extremely good.

Zone I – Our favourite view of the show. It is the perfect distance from Sleeping Beauty Castle and if you position yourself by one of the railings that surround the flowerbeds you will have a near perfect view of the show. Be aware of the large speaker and light poles getting in the way.

Zone J – A very off-centre view with many trees in front meaning poor visibility. This is improved in the winter when there is less foliage and some spots can be decent. When the trees have leaves, this is not an acceptable viewing location.

Zone K – Views are obstructed by trees and the Disney Illuminations control booth. No visibility.

Zone L – Another one of our favourite views of the show; it is a good distance from the castle to see the full show effects whilst not feeling too distant. This area is also usually less crowded than Zone I. After the show finishes, you are also closer to the exit.

Zone M, N and O – These zones are located along Main Street, U.S.A. and provide an average view of the show. The closer you are to the Castle, the better. These zones are usually much less crowded than zones closer to the castle. Be aware that you will likely see many people in front of you with kids on their shoulders.

Zone P – No visibility.

Zone Q – Has to be staked out very early and involves you standing on the bandstand in Town Square – there is very limited space here but it provides an elevated view over other guests on Main street, U.S.A. Specific projections are hard to see from here but the unique view of the show from this location makes it worth considering. It is not the way the show should be experienced the first time you see it, however. At the end of the show, you are right by the park exit and well ahead of the crowds.

Glow with the Show:

You can become part of *Disney Illuminations* with glow-in-the-dark hats, which Disney has dubbed *LightEars*.

They are like the classic Mickey ear shaped hats that you will see in the parks, but with LEDs inside the ears. These LEDs change colour in time with the show, so when the castle is coloured blue the hat on your head will turn blue as well.

They can be purchased at most shopping locations on Main Street, U.S.A for €20 each, as well as from in-park merchandise carts.

The effect, unfortunately, is rather disappointing, with only a dozen guests using the hats each night.

Disney Parades

Disney Stars on Parade is the best way to see all your favourite Disney characters in one place as they parade through Fantasyland, around the castle hub and down Main Street U.S.A.

The parade is performed daily and the time may vary seasonally – it has usually at 5:00pm or 5:30pm for most of the year. Check the in-park Times Guide for the exact schedule.

This is a brand new parade for the 25th Anniversary and debuted in late March 2017.

Characters in the parade may vary from day to day but you can typically see about 50 different characters and floats, including: Tinker Bell, Toy Story characters, Simba, Nala, Baloo, Mowgli, Captain Hook, Peter Pan and characters from Finding Dory.

Other characters include Rapunzel, Cinderella, Snow White, Anna and Elsa.

It's not just the characters which are exciting though - one of the floats is a fire-breathing dragon which is sure to wow visitors.

The most popular place to watch the parade from is Main Street, U.S.A. You should secure your spot about one hour before the parade starts for the best view if watching from here.

The parade is performed regardless of the weather; including during light or moderate rain. During heavy rain, or if there is a thunderstorm alert, there is the potential for the parade to be cancelled or delayed. In either case, an announcement will be made at the parade start time.

Some other Disney theme parks feature a nighttime parade, in addition to a daytime one. Although, Disneyland Paris has done this in the past, this is not currently offered.

During seasonal events such as Spring, Halloween and Christmas, smaller parades with three to five-floats (dubbed cavalcades) are performed several times a day in addition to the main parade.

2017: The 25th Anniversary

The 12th April 2017 is a very exciting date for Disneyland Paris as it marks 25 years since it first opening.

With every major milestone, the park puts on a celebratory event.

Some details of its anniversary celebrations are still under wraps but here is what has been announced so far.

First of all, the 25th anniversary celebration will begin on 26th March 2017. The anniversary events usually last for a full year - in this case until April 2018.

Celebrations are often extended further as the end date approaches. All the extra entertainment is likely to stick around after the 25th anniversary.

Renovated attractions:
Star Tours is upgraded to a 2.0 version; *Space Mountain* gets more comfortable trains and becomes *Hyperspace Mountain* with a Star Wars theme, and *Pirates of the Caribbean* sees the arrival of Jack Sparrow animatronics. This in additional other enhancements such as a new explosive finale at *Big Thunder Mountain*.

At the Studios, *Mickey and the Magician* has replaced *Animagique*. Many other attractions will also be upgraded to improve the quality of the effects and décors inside.

The hotels are also going through a vast renovation program for the 25th celebrations, and beyond.

Star Wars Meet & Greet:
While *Star Tours* is under refurbishment, so is the Star Traders shop. This shop is replaced by a Star Wars character meet and greet.

A New Parade and Shows:
A new daytime parade, called *Disney Stars on Parade* arrives at Disneyland Park. It is a big change from the previous parade, which had been around for ten years.

Two new shows will also debut: *Mickey presents "Happy Anniversary Disneyland Paris"* and *The Starlit Princess Waltz*.

Nighttime Spectacular:
Disney Dreams is replaced by a new nighttime show called *Disney Illuminations*, including scenes from The Little Mermaid, Frozen and the motion pictures of Beauty and the Beast, Star Wars and Pirates of the Caribbean.

Walt Disney Studios Park

Walt Disney Studios Park is the second, and newest, park at Disneyland Paris. Here you can go behind the scenes and experience the magic of the movies.

Walt Disney Studios Park opened in 2002 and has expanded greatly over the years. In general, the park targets adolescents and adults more than young children and contains a number of thrill rides. There are also, of course, several attractions for the younger family members too.

Despite its expansion over the years, you would still be hard-pressed to spend an entire day in Walt Disney Studios Park due to the limited number of attractions. Disneyland Paris has stated that expanding the park and improving its offerings is a priority.

In 2014 *Ratatouille: The Adventure* was unveiled, a unique 3D trackless dark ride, and many more attractions are set to come in the next few years.

At 4.4 million visitors per year, Walt Disney Studios Park is Europe's fifth most popular theme park, but still only receives less than half the number of visitors that its big brother, Disneyland Park, gets next door.

The park is divided into five main areas: Front Lot, Toon Studio, Production Courtyard, Toy Story Playland and Backlot.

Front Lot

As you enter the park, you are in Front Lot. This is both the area with the Fantasia fountain and the covered area with shops and restaurants.

Front Lot is the entrance area to Walt Disney Studios Park, and home to *Disney Studio 1* – an indoor shopping and dining area designed to resemble Hollywood.

Disney Studio 1 is the equivalent of Main Street, U.S.A. in Disneyland Park. The façades of famous Hollywood buildings, as well as all the camera equipment tell that this isn't just a recreation, but a real working set designed to be used when making movies.

Sometimes there are pieces of street entertainment that are performed here. This area often offers face painting too (priced at €10 to €14).

Front Lot is home to Studio Services (Guest Services) where you can get assistance, make a complaint, leave positive feedback and apply for disability assistance cards. It is also home to Shutterbugs, the park's photography studio.

Once you have walked through Studio 1, you will see the Partners Statue with Mickey and Walt Disney holding hands - a great photo opportunity. Front Lot is also commonly home to photo points with Disney characters.

Top Tip: If you are dining at Restaurant En Coulisse, look up - there is seating on the upper floor, which is open during busier times.

DINING:

Restaurant En Coulisse - Counter Service, adult set menus are €12 to €15, children's set menus are priced at €8. This restaurant runs on the right-hand side of Studio 1 behind several façades of famous movie sets.
The Hep Cat Corner - Snacks, serves hot and cold drinks for €3 to €4, a donut and drink is €5.50, ice creams are €3 to €4.

Production Courtyard

Production courtyard is the centre of the park with several attractions.

Attractions

Stitch Live!

🎟️ No	📏 None	📷 No	⊘ 15 minutes	⏳ Until next show

Enter a special transmission room and before you know it, a Cast Member will connect you and your fellow earthlings in your theatre to Stitch and you will be speaking with him live in space.

Stitch is curious about how the planet Earth works, so he will ask all sorts of strange questions to learn about our home.

All in all, this attraction is good fun, although Stitch can sometimes be a bit mean to the adults.

There are separate English and French shows.

Disney Junior: Live on Stage

| FP: No | None | 📷 No | ⌄ 25 minutes | ⏳ Until next show |

Join Mickey, Donald and the gang (represented in puppet form) as they prepare for Minnie's birthday party – but they need your help to succeed.

This toddler-friendly show will have your kids clapping, running around and dancing and is sure to be a highlight for Disney Junior fans.

Separate English and French shows are performed throughout the day; guests can see the next show time outside the attraction, as well as how many seats remain.

Top Tip: Jake (from the Neverland Pirates) & Sofia The First both have meet and greets in the pre-show waiting area.

Studio Tram Tour: Behind the Magic

| FP: No | None | 📷 No | ⌄ 15 minutes | ⏳ 30 to 60 minutes |

Important: Due to the Experience Enhancement Program, this attraction is closed from January 2017 to April 2017.

Hop aboard a studio tram and see authentic props and vehicles from well-known movies, and sets close-up. During the ride you will experience fire, water and earthquakes, and see movie scenes unfold in front of you.

Commentary is provided in English and French via screens on the tram.

This is a great family adventure that everyone can experience. It features a cool Reign of Fire scene, as well as the impressive Catastrophe Canyon.

Kids are unlikely to recognise most of the films, however.

The Twilight Zone: Tower of Terror

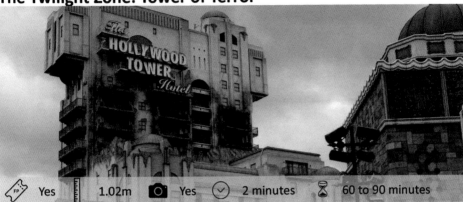

Yes   1.02m   Yes   2 minutes   60 to 90 minutes

The Twilight Zone: Tower of Terror transports you to the fifth dimension as you enter an elevator for the ride of your life.

During this two-minute experience, you will see incredible special effects and feel what it is like to drop 124 feet (38m) straight down over and over again.

Disney summarises the ride nicely: "You are the passengers on a most uncommon elevator about to ascend into your very own episode of...The Twilight Zone."

"One stormy night long ago, five people stepped through the door of an elevator and into a nightmare. That door is opening once again, and this time it's opening for you."

You board a service elevator; learn about the ghostly past of the hotel and then you 'drop in' for yourself.

The elevator is like a free-fall ride, except that you are pulled down faster than gravity causing you to come out of your seat – thank goodness for the seatbelts. The motors on this ride are very powerful and within a split second the elevator changes from going up to down, creating a weightless sensation unlike any other ride.

The atmosphere inside is truly immersive and is possibly the best theming in the whole of Disneyland Paris.

The pre-show is great and you can't help but feel the tension before you plummet.

In addition, the Cast Members who work on this ride really add to the creepy atmosphere with their acting.

This is a fun ride, but it is an intense experience that WILL have you screaming.

Fastpass is recommended as the queue can be long, but be aware that by using Fastpass you will miss out on the detail in the interior queue line.

First time riders should consider buying the on-ride photo for their reactions.

DINING:

Restaurant des Stars – Buffet. The adult price is €33 with one drink; the children's buffet is €18 with one soft drink included. Both buffets are in the Standard Meal Plan. **Hollywood and Lime** – Snack location. Drinks - €3 to €4, desserts - €3 to €4, teatime treats are also available.

Backlot

Backlot is situated in the top-left hand corner of the park. In addition to the attractions below, you can also meet Spider-Man at a permanent location here.

Attractions

Rock 'n' Roller Coaster: Starring Aerosmith

Yes	1.20m	Yes	90 seconds	20 to 45 minutes

Hop aboard a SoundTracker and take a ride through an Aerosmith music video at over 55mph (90km/h) in this high-speed roller coaster.

The ride will take you through three inversions, 4.5Gs of Force and more - and it all starts with a catapult launch to the maximum speed in under 2.5 seconds.

In the pre-show you will see lifelike holograms of Aerosmith preparing for a music video - you're going to get in on the fun.

After meeting the band, watch the trains launch to their top speed in just a few seconds.

For each launch there is a short light show, fog and a countdown. This launch looks much more intimidating than it actually feels, in our opinion.

Each SoundTracker ride vehicle is fitted with speakers all around your body including around your head for ultimate musical enjoyment. There are several inversions, but the ride is incredibly smooth and comfortable.

Each vehicle plays a different set of Aerosmith songs from the song list. The lights and effects on the ride change colour and sequence depending on your vehicle too.

Rock 'n' Roller Coaster almost always has surprisingly low wait times, even when the rest of the park is relatively packed. Coaster fans: do it!

Top Tip 1: Keep your head against the headrest for the launch to avoid whiplash.

Top Tip 2: When park attendance is low, Fastpass is not offered for this attraction.

Top Tip 3: Wait times peak significantly throughout the day as the *Moteurs... Action* stunt show, located right next door, finishes and dumps 3000 guests at a time into the park.

Moteurs, Action! Stunt Show Spectacular

No	None	No	40 minutes	Until next show

At *Moteurs, Action!* sit back and watch movie stunts be performed in front of your very eyes – and then learn how they are done!

This attraction is a major draw for many of Disneyland Paris' visitors and pulls in thousands of guests at a time, meaning that queues for other attractions are shorter when the show is being performed.

Arrive around 30 minutes before show-time to get a good seat - the middle seating section provides the best view and the lower down you are, the closer you are to the action.

Although all seats do have a good view, being closer to the action makes the experience even more enjoyable.

Armageddon: Les Effets Speciaux

No	None	No	20 minutes	Less than 20 minutes

Armageddon is what the Walt Disney Studios Park is all about - getting you to experience what it is like to be in a film.

Here, you are on the set of 'Armageddon' on the Russian Space Station. Your job as an extra is to act and scream as directed as you are plunged into space.

During the pre-show, you will rehearse with the director as you watch various scenes from the film. Then, you are taken to the Space Station set.

Once on the "hot set", right on cue a meteor shower hits the space station and the adventure begins.

Warning: Once the meteor shower starts you should be ready for collapsing ceilings, loud noises, sparks, fire, water, a dropping floor and much more. This is an intense experience. Avoid the centre area and the two doors on the side of the set if you, or your kids, are easily startled.

DINING:

Cafe des Cascadeurs – Table/Quick Service Hybrid. Salads are €8.50, adult set menus are €13 to €15, children's menus are €9. Drinks, desserts and ice cream are also served.
Blockbuster Cafe – Quick Service. A la carte sandwiches are priced at €7, pizzas are €9, salads and pasta are €7 to €8, drinks and desserts are also served and priced between €3 and €4.

Toon Studio

Discover the magic behind Disney cartoons and animation in this area of the park, from Disney classics to Pixar favourites.

Attractions

Crush's Coaster

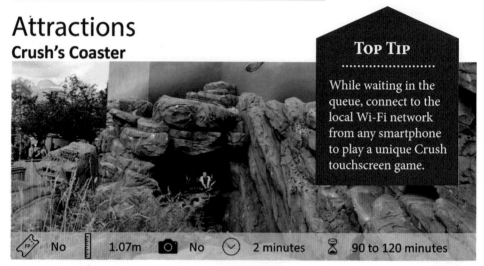

TOP TIP

While waiting in the queue, connect to the local Wi-Fi network from any smartphone to play a unique Crush touchscreen game.

No	1.07m	No	2 minutes	90 to 120 minutes

Journey through the East Australian Current with Crush in this fast and thrilling coaster.

Crush's Coaster is a unique attraction and the only of its kind in any Disney theme park worldwide.

Guests board turtle shells in groups of four, sat back-to-back in pairs. The ride starts off relatively calmly as a dark ride with scenes but it soon begins to build pace as the cars begin their high-speed roller coaster sequence.

Most of the roller coaster portion is in darkness with effects scattered around the track to give you the feeling of riding the waves with Crush.

Although the ride may seem to target younger kids, do not be fooled - this is a wild, fast adventure so read the warning signs outside first.

Some guests rate this as the most "thrilling" ride in the whole of Disneyland Paris, so it is a definite must-do for thrill seekers!

The popularity of the characters and the ride's low hourly capacity, means that this ride regularly has the second longest queue in the entire park, after Ratatouille. The ride does not offer Fastpass.

Ride Crush's Coaster first thing in the morning or just before park closing for the shortest waits.

Even on less busy days, queues exceed 40 minutes and it is common to see the wait at over 90 minutes.

We recommend that you queue up for Crush when the park pre-opens at 9:30am – it is really the only way to do it without waiting for a long time. Just before park closing, a long wait time is often displayed to discourage people from getting in the queue line.

Top Tip: A Single Rider queue is available; the wait time posted for this is often exaggerated so that guests choose to use the regular queue and the Single Rider line does not get too long.

Art of Animation

 No None No 20 minutes Less than 30 minutes

If you fancy seeing more behind the scenes magic and learning about how Disney films are animated, this is the place to visit.

The first pre-show room of this attraction tells the history of how animation has evolved with models, videos, and replicas of animation equipment.

Here you have a chance to see one of only two multi-plane cameras in the world. These were used to create some of the original Disney classics and they are true masterpieces.

Also in this room, a large screen plays a video with Roy O Disney explaining these machines.

Next, you are ushered into a cinema room where you will see a collection of clips showing how animated films can create emotions within their audience.

Next, you enter another room with a live animator who will guide you through how Disney characters are created from scratch to the final product – Mushu, the dragon from *Mulan*, is also on hand to help.

The final room contains several props and paintings.

This room allows you to exit back into park – alternatively you can stick around for one of the drawing classes where an animator will teach you to draw one of the Disney characters. Pencils and paper are provided and you get to take your efforts home with you. These drawing classes are only available seasonally and at specific times, but are great fun to take part in.

Sometimes character meet and greets are available in this final room too.

Top Tip: If you want to take part in a drawing class without doing the whole attraction, enter through the shop selling Disney artwork on the side of the building.

Animagique Theater – "Mickey and the Magician"

 No None No 30 minutes Until next show

Formerly the home of *Animagique*, a blacklight stage show, this theatre now hosts a new stage show - *Mickey and the Magician*.

Go back in time to Paris at the turn of the 19th century... and enter a great Magician's workshop, where the assistant is no other than a certain Mickey Mouse!

As well as the main cheese himself, you can expect appearances from Tinker Bell from *Peter Pan*, Lumière from *Beauty and the Beast*, the Genie from *Aladdin*, the Fairy Godmother from *Cinderella*, Rafiki from *The Lion King*, and even Elsa from *Frozen*.

With unforgettable songs such as "Let it Go" and "Friend like Me", this show is an unmissable spectacular that we think is the best show that Disneyland Paris has ever done - it is of West End theatre quality.

The show runs until 8th January 2017. It will then return from 18th March 2017 to 3rd September 2017. We expect the show to continue running after this date but Disneyland Paris has not made any announcements.

Flying Carpets over Agrabah

FP Yes	None	No	90 seconds	Less than 30 minutes

Board one of Aladdin's flying carpets and get ready to fly over Agrabah. As you soar through the skies you will hear the Genie through his director's megaphone telling you how to act.

The ride itself is a simple spinner ride, and is very similar to both *Dumbo* and *Orbitron* (at Disneyland Park) – this ride, however, often has much shorter queues.

Here you can raise and lower your carpet, as well as tilt it backwards and forwards!

Top Tip: It is very rare for the Fastpass machines to be activated on this ride.

Cars Quatre Roues Rallye

FP No	None	No	90 seconds	30 to 60 minutes

Hop in for the spin of your life on Route 66 with the characters from Disney Pixar's *Cars*.

The queue line is filled with details immersing you into the world of Radiator Springs.

There are even life-size models of Lightning McQueen and Mater for photos.

The ride is very similar to the teacups ride in Disneyland Park but you spin a little faster in this version, and it always

looks like you are going to collide with the other cars, which adds to the fun.

Vehicles can accommodate up to 2 adults, plus 2 extra kids.

Ratatouille: The Adventure

Yes   None   No   5 minutes   90 to 120 minutes

Launched in Summer 2014, *Ratatouille: The Adventure* is the newest ride at Disneyland Paris and an innovative one at that. It is suitable for the whole family.

Here you board a 'ratmobile' and travel through the streets of Paris, scurrying along rooftops and kitchens in a clever 4D immersive ride.

Along your journey you will be immersed in all directions - your 3D glasses put you in the heart of the action as you approach giant projection screens.

You can also expect to feel the heat from a grill, the cold of a refrigerator, and you may even get splashed once or twice. There are even different smells throughout.

The *Ratatouille* ride vehicles do not follow a track, taking slightly different paths for a unique experience each time.

As it is the newest attraction, this ride has the longest waits of the entire resort, and Fastpasses run out very quickly – usually within 30 minutes of park opening.

At park closing, an inflated wait time is often displayed to discourage people from queuing.

A Single Rider Line is available for this attraction. This will typically reduce wait times to less than 30 minutes - often the wait is less than 15 minutes. On extremely busy days the wait for Single Rider may reach 60 minutes.

When disembarking your 'ratmobile' and returning your 3D glasses, look ahead for a glimpse into *Bistrot Chez Remy*, a restaurant where you are shrunk down to the size of a rat. More information on this dining location is available in the box below.

DINING:

Bistrot Chez Remy – Table Service. Set menus only. The price is €32 for 2 courses (no dessert), €40 for 3 courses with the Emile Menu, €48 for 2 courses (no dessert) from a wider selection, or €60 for the Menu Gusteau - 3 courses with premium choices. A kids menu is €18 and a Premium Kids Menu is €32. The Gusteau menu and the Premium Kids Menu are on the Premium Meal Plan. The standard kids menu and the Emile Menu are on the Plus Meal Plan. This is the only Table Service restaurant in Walt Disney Studios Park and advanced reservations are strongly recommended year-round.

Toy Story Playland

Toy Story Playland shrinks you down to the size of a toy in Andy's back yard.

Attractions

Toy Soldiers Parachute Drop

🎟 No	▯ 0.81m	📷 No	✓ 1 minute	⧖ 60 to 90 minutes

Board one of the Toy Soldiers' parachutes and get ready to soar up into the sky and then glide back down to the ground again and again.

This is a great family ride and has become a new rite of passage for many.

Queues can get extremely long for this ride, so get here early.

Top Tip: A Single Rider queue line is available for guests wishing to board individually.

Slinky Dog Zigzag Spin

🎟 No	▯ None	📷 No	✓ 90 seconds	⧖ 20 to 45 minutes

Hop on Slinky Dog and enjoy yourself as you spin round and round in circles getting increasingly faster

and faster.

This is a fun family-friendly attraction that is likely to

entertain everyone from young toddlers to parents.

RC Racer

No | 1.20m | No | 1 minute | 60 to 90 minutes

Hop on the RC car from Pixar's Toy Story films, and feel the wind in your hair as you ride both forwards and backwards along the car track.

The ride is great fun and a good adrenaline rush – it is often likened to the swinging pirate ships found at many theme parks, but we prefer the feeling on this.

Here, you are also secured by overhead harnesses, which you aren't on a pirate ship.

At the highest point, riders are 24m (80ft) high and the free-fall feeling backwards is great fun.

The ride looks significantly more intimidating than it actually is and the sensation is not anywhere near as scary as it looks, in our opinion.

RC Racer has one of the most boring, and tedious, queues in all the park so we would recommend avoiding it if waits are long. It also moves very slowly.

Top Tip: A Single Rider queue is available for guests wishing to save time and board individually. Unfortunately, to get to this queue you may have to wait in the normal queue line for a good while until the split point. This is because the Single Rider line only starts half-way into the regular queue.

Get here early to ride this attraction, as queues build up quickly and the ride has a dismal hourly capacity - the lowest for any ride in the park.

PARADES AND FIREWORKS AT WALT DISNEY STUDIOS PARK:

Live entertainment at Walt Disney Studios Park is limited to the stage shows on offer such as *Mickey and the Magician* and *Moteurs, Action.*

Unfortunately, this park does not have a daytime or nighttime parade, nor does it have a nighttime show or fireworks. You will find the nightly fireworks show at Disneyland Park.

Exceptions: There is a firework show offered for guests at this park for the transition from New Year's Eve to New Year's Day at midnight. During *Season of the Force* in early 2017, there will be a nighttime Star Wars-themed spectacular projected onto *The Twilight Zone: Tower of Terror*'s building façades.

Fastpass

Many theme parks allows guests to skip long queue lines for a fee, but Disneyland Paris offers its unique Fastpass system at no cost. Fastpass allows you to reserve a time slot for select attractions in advance, come back at an appointed time, and ride with little to no wait. While waiting for your Fastpass reservation time, you can do something else such as shop, dine, watch a show or experience another attraction.

How to use Fastpass

❶ Find a Fastpass ride
You can identify rides that offer Fastpass by the *FP* logo on park maps. It is helpful to know which attractions offer Fastpass in advance by reading through this guide and looking at our park maps at the back.

❷ Check the wait time and decide
At a FP-enabled attraction, there are ride entrances – the *stand-by* entrance where you can queue up and ride (e.g. 45-minute wait), and the *Fastpass* entrance.

If the standby wait time is short, use the regular standby entrance. If the wait is too long for you, then you should use the FP system. If the standby wait is less than 30 minutes, we recommend you wait in the standby line and not use FP. This is because FPs often require you to backtrack across the park negating any time savings.

❸ Get your Fastpass
Near the ride entrance is the FP distribution area with large machines and a screen showing the current return time for FP reservations (e.g. 14:15 to 14:45). This is the time your reservation is made for, and will be printed on your FP.

Go to the FP machines and swipe or scan your park ticket or annual pass on the reader. The machine will print a paper FP telling you what time your reservation is for. This is the same time window that was shown on the screen above the entrance. Keep your FP and park ticket safe.

❹ Wait
Dine, explore the park or enjoy another ride or show until your FP return time.

❺ Return and Ride
Return to the ride during the time window on your FP, entering through the ride's Fastpass entrance. Hand your FP to the Cast Member at the Fastpass entrance who will keep it. Now, you can ride within a few minutes, skipping the regular queue – the wait time with a Fastpass is often under 5 minutes but can be up to 15 minutes.

Fastpass Tickets

FASTPASS®
Valable entre
Enter Between

18:00
ET / AND
18:30

Un autre ticket FASTPASS®
sera disponible apres
16:40

Another FASTPASS® ticket
will be available after
16:40

05/10/2008

15/10/2008 4052010113250018924O2   14:43

This is an example of a Disneyland Paris Fastpass.

The top of the ticket states your return time - marked as "Enter Between". This is the 30-minute time slot you should return to the attraction at. In this case it is 18:00 to 18:30.

Next, your ticket will tell you what time you can get another Fastpass – in this case 16:40.

Finally, the ticket shows today's date. Remember your Fastpass is only valid on the day it is issued.

The Fastpass System Explained

Now that you have read about the wonder of the Fastpass system, you may think that you can get a Fastpass for each ride and completely avoid queues. This is not possible.

Firstly, not every ride offers Fastpass - only 10 rides out of 60 offer this service. Secondly, you can only hold one Fastpass ticket at a time - there are exceptions to this is you will read on the next page.

Therefore, you will use Fastpass throughout your day at Disneyland Paris but only once in a while.

How the system works:
Every Disneyland Paris entry ticket and annual pass includes Fastpass access – it is a free system open to every guest.

Each day, Team Leaders will decide what percentage of riders they want to be able to use the Fastpass system. Let's say that in this case it is 50%.

So, assuming *Big Thunder Mountain* can handle 2000 guests per hour, the Fastpass system will distribute 1000 Fastpass tickets for each operating hour. That means 50% of guests will use Fastpass to board and 50% will use the standby queue each hour.

There are, therefore, a limited number of Fastpass tickets for each ride each hour. This is to ensure that the standby queue line is kept to a reasonable level.

The first Fastpass return time for an attraction is usually 30 minutes after park opening, sometimes longer.

Fastpass slots then move in 5 minute increments so after all the Fastpasses for 10:30am-11:00am are distributed, the next return time will be 10:35am-11:05am. Once all Fastpasses have been distributed for the day, the machines are shut down.

Rides may not offer Fastpasses for the entire park operating hours for operational reasons.

If you want to know what time the last Fastpass return time is for, ask the Cast Members at the attraction. When Fastpass stops being used, the regular queue usually moves twice as quickly.

Due to the limited number of Fastpasses, tickets run out on popular rides early in the day. This happens often on *Peter Pan's Flight, Big Thunder Mountain, Buzz Lightyear Laser Blast* and *Ratatouille: The Adventure.*

On busy days these rides will distribute their daily allocation of Fastpasses by lunchtime. *Ratatouille* regularly distributes all its Fastpass tickets within 30 minutes of the park opening.

Is Fastpass always available?
Most rides offer Fastpass daily. Others only offer Fastpasses when there are a certain number of guests in the park.

Rides that may not have Fastpasses in off-peak times are: *Star Tours, Indiana Jones et le Temple du Peril, Rock 'n' Roller Coaster: Starring Aerosmith* and *Flying Carpets over Agrabah.*

Good to Know:
Tower of Terror and *Rock 'n' Roller Coaster* both have a compulsory pre-show video. After this, you enter a short queue line to board the ride vehicle itself but the wait can be up to 15 minutes.

Buzz Lightyear, Star Wars Hyperspace Mountain and *Ratatouille* also often have a 15-minute wait before boarding with Fastpass.

On other attractions ,you should be on the ride in less than five minutes with a Fastpass.

Get extra Fastpasses

Officially you can only hold one Fastpass at a time. However, there are exceptions.

• When your Fastpass return time begins, you can get another Fastpass even if you have not used your current Fastpass yet. E.g. You have a *Star Tours* Fastpass for 14:00-14:30. It is 14:05. You can get another Fastpass from 14:00.

• Cast Members (at their discretion) usually allow you to use a Fastpass after the return time, though not before. This is not allowed at *Ratatouille*.

• The Fastpass system is not connected between the two theme parks. Therefore, you can hold a Fastpass for a Walt Disney Studios Park rude and another for a Disneyland Park ride simultaneously.

Know that it can be a 20 to 30-minute walk from the back of one park to the other. You must have a 2-park 'hopper' ticket to enter both parks on the same day.

• If your return time is over two hours away, you can get a second Fastpass two hours after you picked up the first. E.g. You got a *Star Wars Hyperspace*

Mountain Fastpass at 10:00; the return time is 15:00-15:30. As 15:00 is over two hours away from when you got your Fastpass, you can get another Fastpass at 12:00 (two hours after 10:00). Check when your next Fastpass is available on the bottom of your latest Fastpass ticket.

• The *Indiana Jones* and *Star Tours* Fastpasses are not linked with the rest of the Fastpass system. This means you can hold a Fastpass for either of these two attractions AND another Disneyland Park Fastpass at the same time.

List of Fastpass attractions

Disneyland Park:
• *Star Wars Hyperspace Mountain*
• *Buzz Lightyear Laser Blast*
• *Star Tours*
• *Peter Pan's Flight*
• *Indiana Jones et le Temple du Peril*
• *Big Thunder Mountain*

Walt Disney Studios Park:
• *The Twilight Zone: Tower of Terror*
• *Rock 'n' Roller Coaster: Starring Aerosmith*
• *Flying Carpets over Agrabah*
• *Ratatouille: The Adventure*

UNIQUE HOTEL FASTPASSES:

• Guests staying in suites at the Disneyland Hotel, Newport Bay Club Hotel, Hotel New York and Sequoia Lodge Hotel get one **VIP Fastpass** per guest. Castle Club guests at the Disneyland Hotel also get this privilege. A VIP Fastpass offers instant, unlimited entry through the Fastpass line of every Fastpass attraction. With a VIP Fastpass, you do not need the standard Fastpass system. You need only show the VIP Fastpass at the entrance to each Fastpass ride to access the Fastpass queue line without a Fastpass reservation. You use the standard queues at non-Fastpass attractions.

• Guests of the Golden Forest Club (Sequoia Lodge Hotel), Compass Club (Newport Bay Club Hotel) and all rooms at the Disneyland Hotel (excluding suites and Castle Club), are given one **Hotel Fastpass** per person per day. This allows guests to access one Fastpass attraction per day through the Fastpass queue instantly. The Hotel Fastpass is valid all day except between 13:00 and 16:00 and is surrendered upon use.

Disney Village

Disney Village is an entertainment district located just next to the theme parks and on-site hotels where you can continue the fun into the night after the parks close. This area houses a live show, a cinema multiplex, restaurants, shops, bars and more. Admission to Disney Village is free.

Entertainment

Buffalo Bill's Wild West Show

Located at the entrance to Disney Village, *Buffalo Bill's* is a dinner show starring Mickey and the gang as they venture through the Wild West. The show lasts 90 minutes and features live animals, Disney characters, a fun atmosphere, stunts and some great decor and sets!

The show is a great way to spend an evening, combining live entertainment and a meal in one place.

Pricing:
Category one seating is priced at £60/€75, and category two seating is £48/€60 per adult. Children's prices are approximately £12/€13 less per person.

To put that into perspective, you should compare the cost of the show to a visit to the theatre it is actually great value – here you get a show, a meal, and a souvenir for one price.

Category 2 is further away the action than Category 1.

Category 1 seating also includes a non-alcoholic welcome cocktail, and treats with your tea or coffee at dessert time.

The food:
The adult meal consists of a roast chicken drumstick, sausage, potato wedges, ice cream and unlimited drink refills (beer or non-alcoholic drinks), as well as dessert and tea and coffee.

There is a separate kids menu. All the food and drinks are included in the price and this is served family-style. The food offered is subject to change.

There are two showings per night – at 18:30 and 21:30 – and the show only operates on select days each week.

More information:
If you are allergic to dust or animals, do not attend this show.

Access to minors (under 18) is not permitted unless they are accompanied by an adult.

Alcohol will only be served for guests aged 18 or over – ID may be required.

Panoramagique

Soar into the sky and get a bird's-eye view of Disneyland Paris from the world's largest helium-filled passenger balloon – *Panoramagique*.

This is a great way to take some photos of the resort where you can clearly see all the land around you, including both theme parks, Disney Village and the resort hotels.

It truly is a unique perspective from where you can appreciate all the different activities on offer at the resort.

Pricing is €12 per adult and €6 per child for the flight. A meal deal which includes a flight on *Panoramagique* and a meal at *Earl of Sandwich* is also available.

Note that flights do not operate in periods of high wind, or adverse weather conditions.

La Marina

La Marina offers water activities from rowing boats to pedal boats, and electric boats to hydro bikes. Non-water activities are also available such as surrey bikes which you can hire. Activities operate at a charge and based on weather conditions.

Operating times are 16:00 to 22:00 daily during high season (school holidays) and on weekends. Activities may also be available at other times.

Pricing:
* *Electric boat hire* – €20 for 20 minutes, 5 people maximum per boat
* *Hydro Bikes* – €5 for 20 minutes, 1 person per bike. Minimum age: 12.
* *Pedal Boats* – €10 for 20 minutes, 5 people maximum per boat.
* *Surrey bike* – €10 for 20 minutes for a 2-adult + 1 child bike, or €15 for 20 minutes for a 4-adult + 1 child bike.

MORE ENTERTAINMENT:
• **Disney Stadium** - In between the Disney Store and the Sports Bar, the Disney Stadium is where you can choose from a series of classic arcade-style video games, as well as air-hockey. Games are mostly priced at €2 each.
• **Sports Bar** - Being at Disneyland Paris does not mean missing out on your favourite sporting. Go to the Sports Bar and watch the game on the huge screen, whilst having a drink or two and a snack. The Sports Bar also hosts weekly karaoke sessions and other forms of live entertainment open to all at no cost.
• **Billy Bob's** - As well as a restaurant during the day, Billy Bob's is a bar and nightclub when the night draws in. Children are allowed in at all times of the day and night, except during some adult-only events. The bar is often frequented by Cast Members at the end of a hard day's work in the parks – here drinks are free-flowing and adults and children alike can dance the night away.
• **Cinema Gaumont** - With 15 different auditoriums, including one with an IMAX screen, there is bound to be something for you to enjoy watching at this cinema. You can check film schedules in advance at http://bit.ly/dlpcinema. Films listed as VOST are shown in their original language (often English) with French subtitles.

Dining

Disney Village has a variety of dining options, including Quick Service (fast food), to Character Dining options (Disney characters visit each table while you eat) to the more traditional Table Service restaurants (order from a menu and your food is brought by a waiter).

McDonald's – Quick Service. McDonald's is a well-known fast food joint and this branch has inflated prices to make up for the location. A standard meal costs between €8 and €9, with a child's meal costing about €5. Be aware that queues can be long if you do not use the automated terminals and want to order from an employee instead. The terminals can be set to English easily and accept bank cards, so we highly recommend these.

Starbucks Coffee – Quick Service. This is a standard Starbucks location but it should be noted that Starbucks is not cheap in France and this location is no different. A hot or cold brewed drink is priced between €4 and €6, and sandwiches are about €5.

Earl of Sandwich – Quick Service. Prices are about €7 for a "gourmet" heated sandwich, and €8 for a salad. The adult sandwich set menu is €11.50, with a kids' set menu at €7.50.

An "Adult Balloon Flight" meal is available for €18.50 and includes a warm sandwich, crisps, a soft drink or bottle of water, a chocolate brownie or cookie, and one flight on *Panoramagique*. A "Child Balloon Flight" meal is €10.50 and includes a mini-sandwich, a soft drink or bottle of water, a mini chocolate brownie or fruit cup, and one flight aboard Panoramagique.

Cafe Mickey – Character Table Service. Breakfast (at 08:00 and 09:30 daily) is €25 for non-Disney hotel guests and €17 for Disney hotel guests as an upgrade to the regular hotel breakfast. Adult lunch and dinner set menus are €36 for 2 courses and €46 for 3 courses without a drink. The children's set menu is €23 including one drink. No *a la carte* at this restaurant - set menus only. Adult and child set menus are both included in the Plus Meal Plan. This meal can be pre-paid and pre-booked if booking a package through Disneyland Paris.

Annette's Diner – Table Service. The American-style breakfast menu is €14. There are several all-day set menus at €20, €30 and €37. The children's set menu is €17.50. Main courses are €17 to €27 a la carte. Milkshakes are €10 to €11. A take-away set menu is €19. The children's set menu and €37 adult set menu are both on the Plus Meal Plan.

King Ludwig's Castle – Table Service. Here there is a special lunch menu (dish of the day style) served until 5:00pm priced at €15. There are also standard menus at €23.50 and €26.50 with no drinks. Main courses are between €16.50 and €27 a la carte.

Planet Hollywood – Table Service. Main courses are €15 to €33. The kids' set menu is €12.50.

Rainforest Cafe – Table Service with a unique rainforest-like ambience. Main courses are €19 to €33. The 2-course set menu is €24.

The Steakhouse – Table Service. Adult set menus are €32, €38 and €43. A la carte menu items are €27 to €60. The children's menu is €18. The children's set menu and the €38 adult set menu are both in the Plus Meal Plan.

New York Style Sandwiches – Quick Service and snack location. The set menus are €10 to €15. The children's menu is €8.50. This location also serves hot and cold drinks, and ice creams.

Billy Bob's Country Western Saloon – Billy Bob's is divided into two dining establishments –

Bar Snacks, a snack and Quick Service location, and *La Grange*, an all-you-can-eat Tex Mex buffet. The bar snacks set menu is €14 for adults and €8 for children. A la carte items are €2.50 to €9.50. The La Grange buffet is €33 with one drink, and €18 per child with one drink. The adult buffet and the children's buffet are both on the Standard meal plan.

Sports Bar – Quick Service and Snacks. Snacks are served until 11:00pm. Sandwiches and burgers are €9 to €11. Other selected warm dishes include pasta bolognese, hot dogs and fish and

chips priced between €8 and €11. Pizzas are €12 to €14. An adult sports bar menu is €14, along with a children's menu at €8.

New: Vapiano – Quick service. Amazingly fresh food. Pick a seat, then order your pizza or pasta made fresh in front of you in minutes. By far our favourite fast food location at the whole resort. Main courses are €11 to €14.

New: Five Guys Burgers – Quick service. The best burgers at Disneyland Paris in our opinion. Expect to pay €6 to €10 for a burger. Fries and drinks are extra.

Shopping

After a meal, you may want to treat yourself with a little bit of retail therapy; here you are spoilt for choice with several merchandise locations.

World of Disney – As you walk into Disney Village from the parks this is the first store you see. *World Of Disney* is the best place to get your Disney merchandise outside of the parks. It is also the largest store at the entire resort, featuring a beautiful interior, plenty of tills to pay at, and a good selection of merchandise.

The Disney Store – This classic location is a traditional-style Disney store. Uniquely, here you can create your own lightsabers, and your own

Mr. Potatohead figure, as well as purchase from a selection of more common Disney merchandise.

Planet Hollywood Store – Get items with the Planet Hollywood brand on them. This store mainly stocks apparel.

The Disney Gallery – This location features collector's items such as figurines and paintings. In addition, you can take advantage of Disney's *Art on Demand* kiosks where you can order a poster from an interactive display, which is created to your specifications and delivered to your home. With over 200 different posters to choose from, there is bound to be something for everyone.

LEGO Store – This is the largest LEGO store in Europe, and a relatively new addition to Disney Village. It features all kinds of different LEGO sets, but unfortunately it does not feature any exclusive Disney-themed merchandise. Nevertheless, it is worth a visit.

Disney Fashion – For fans of Disney clothing, this is your haven.

World of Toys – This store seems to mainly target girls and is *the* place to buy princess dresses, dolls, and sweets.

Rainforest Café Store – The perfect place to get all your Rainforest Café branded merchandise.

Touring Plans

Touring plans are easy to follow guides that minimise your waiting time in queue lines throughout the day. By following them, you can maximise your time in the parks and experience more attractions. There are several different touring plans available to suit your needs.

In order to see all of Disneyland Park you will need to allow at least two days. However, you *can* hit the headline attractions at the park in just one day if you are pressed for time. Walt Disney Studios Park can be seen in one day comfortably.

Unless you are going during an off-peak season, you will be hard pressed to see the highlights from both parks in one day – there is simply not enough time.

These touring plans are definitely not set in stone, so feel free to adapt them to suit the needs of your party. It is important to note that these plans focus on experiencing the rides; if your focus is on meeting all the characters or seeing

all the shows, then a touring plan is unlikely to be suitable for you. The only way to minimise waits for characters is to get to the parks and meet and greets early.

These touring plans are intense BUT you will get to cram in as much as possible during your visit. If you are at the resort for multiple days, feel free to follow the plans at a more leisurely pace. In addition, if you do not want to experience a particular ride, simply skip that step but do not change the order of the steps.

Do remember that until mid-2017, there will be a number of attractions closed for enhancement. Skip these steps if they are shut when you visit.

You must purchase your tickets in advance to make the most of your time and these touring plans. If you need to buy them on the day, turn up at least 30 minutes earlier than the start times recommended on these plans - and even earlier during peak season.

Insider Tip: In order to minimise the time you spend waiting in queue lines, you will often need to cross the park from one side to the other – this is purposely done by theme parks to disperse crowds more evenly. Note for example how the three roller coasters at Disneyland Park are all in different lands and far away from each other – the same also applies at Walt Disney Studios Park.

Disneyland Park

1 Day Plan for Guests with Extra Magic Hours:

Step 1: At 7:50am be at the park gates for entry - the park opens at 8:00am. Pick up a Park Map and a Times Guide under the archways of Main Street, U.S.A. Station. These list parade, show, character and firework times, as well as attraction closures. If you want to meet any characters do so now, before the rides. Walk down Main Street, U.S.A., get photos and proceed straight to *Sleeping Beauty Castle*.

Step 2: Decide whether you want to prioritise thrill rides or kids rides. If you want thrills, enter Discoveryland and ride *Star Wars Hyperspace Mountain*, followed by *Buzz Lightyear Laser Blast*. If you want kids rides, enter Fantasyland and ride *Dumbo: The Flying Elephant* first, followed by *Peter Pan's Flight*.

Step 3: If you arrive at the park for opening and Extra Magic Hours run for two hours, it should now be 8:45am at the very latest, and you have plenty of time to do other attractions.

Although there is not a specific list of rides that are open during EMHs, you still have enough time to experience the following attractions provided they are open: *Mad Hatter's Tea Cups, Le Carousel de*

Lancelot and *Orbitron: Machines Volantes*.

You should easily be able to do all of the Extra Magic Hours rides before the rest of the park opens at 10:00am. Explore *Sleeping Beauty Castle* and its interior if you have time.

Step 4: By 9:50am, make your way back to the park's hub in front of the castle. Here, wait at the entrance to Frontierland with other guests.

Step 5: At 10:00am, when the park opens, go directly to *Big Thunder Mountain*. Ride it.

Step 6: Now it is decision time again – What do you fancy doing? a) Driving a car or b) Meeting the Disney Princesses. If you fancy driving a car, walk over to *Autopia* in Discoveryland. Otherwise, visit *Princess Pavilion* in Fantasyland. Be prepared

for a wait at both of these.

Step 7: Next decision: Do you fancy meeting Mickey Mouse, or going on a simulator ride into outer space? *Meet Mickey Mouse* in Fantasyland is the permanent home for the big cheese himself. Or for the space adventurers it is time to ride *Star Tours* in Discoveryland (closed until March 2017).

Step 8: Now is your chance to do any rides you have opted not to do so far. If, for example, you opted to go to *Autopia* and *Star Tours*, then now is the time to go to *Meet Mickey Mouse* and *Princess Pavilion* (or vice-versa). Queues for these attractions will only continue to increase into the evening hours. Also, meet and greet locations shut several hours before the park closes.

Step 9: It should now be time to grab some lunch.

Step 10: You now have a few rides left to do in Fantasyland. Experience *Casey Junior, Le Pays des Contes de Fees, Blanche Neige (Snow White)* and *Pinocchio*. Ride these one after another, in this order, if you want to do them all. *Casey Junior* and *Storybook* close several hours before the rest of the park.

Step 11: If any live shows such as *Frozen Sing-Along* or *Forest of Enchantment* are playing during your visit, you may want to watch these now.

Step 12: Is it time for the Parade yet? The parade is traditionally at 5:30pm but make sure to check your Times Guide for exact timings. Show up 45 minutes before or even earlier for a good spot on Main Street, U.S.A.

Step 12: Many people leave after the parade, so the park will become less busy. Now is the time to either take a bit of a rest on a bench to avoid burning out or to go on rides that have fast moving queues. Ride *Pirates of the Caribbean*.

Step 13: Ride *"it's a small world"*. This attraction handles thousands of guests an hour, so queues are always moving.

Step 14: Ride *Indiana Jones et le Temple du Peril*.

Step 15: Head to *Phantom Manor*. Do not forget to explore the cemetery located by the ride exit for some great puns.

Step 16: Check when the night-time show *Disney Illuminations* is being presented. This should not to be missed!

Now depending on what time of the day it is, and when the park closes, it is either time to watch *Disney Illuminations*, have dinner or do the walkthrough attractions.

Walkthrough attractions do not have a waiting time. These include: *Adventure Isle and La Cabane des Robinson, Le Passage Enchante d'Aladdin, Alice's Curious Labyrinth* (closes early for the fireworks), and the wonderfully themed *Les Mystères de Nautilus*.

Step 17: Get a spot in front of the castle or on Main Street, U.S.A. at least 30 to 60 minutes before *Disney Illuminations* begins. See our section on *Disney Illuminations* at the end of the Disneyland Park chapter for help finding the perfect spot. We grab a hot dog from Casey's Corner whilst waiting to help the time pass.

Disneyland Park Touring Plan Notes

Two attractions that not covered in these plans:
• *Thunder Mesa Riverboat Landing* - The wait time for this attraction is never longer than 30 minutes so you may be able to fit it in.
• *Disneyland Railroad* goes around the park. There are four different stations to board at, but the one with the shortest queues is usually Frontierland station as it is hidden away. Be aware that the railroad often stops operation before most

other rides in the park.

Disneyland Paris also lists the following as attractions so you might want to fit them in at some point:

• *Horse-Drawn Streetcars*
• *Main Street Vehicles*
• The *Liberty* and *Discovery Arcades*

We do not feel these warrant the time spent on them, unless you have time to spare.

This guide does not take into account live shows, as those vary throughout the year, check your Times Guide for more. Be sure to watch them.

Also be sure to visit the *Gallery* inside Sleeping Beauty Castle (upstairs) and the *Dragon's Lair* underneath. Entry to Sleeping Beauty Castle ceases at least one hour before Disney Illuminations, as does all of Fantasyland.

1 DAY WITHOUT EXTRA MAGIC HOURS - FOCUS: KIDS RIDES

Step 1: Arrive at 9:20am at Disneyland Park's entrance. Enter the park when it pre-opens at 9:30am. Until 10:00am you can shop, eat and ride the *Main Street Vehicles*. Pick up a Park Guide and a Times Guide under the archways of *Main Street U.S.A. Station*. These contain parade, show, character and firework times, as well as attraction closures and park hours.

Step 2: Walk down Main Street, U.S.A., get photos and proceed straight to *Sleeping Beauty Castle*.

At Sleeping Beauty Castle's hub lies the entrance to all the lands of the park – Fantasyland and Discoveryland will be open to Disney Hotel guests and some Annual Passholders at this time. Other lands will be cordoned off.

Stand by the rope leading to the castle. This rope is removed at 10:00am so all guests can go through.

Step 3: Ride *Dumbo: The Flying Elephant*. It will have long waits later.

Step 4: Get a *Peter Pan's Flight* Fastpass.

Step 5: Go to *Princess Pavilion* to meet a princess.

Step 6: Go to *Meet Mickey Mouse*.

Step 7: Ride *Casey Junior*.

Step 8: Ride *Le Pays des Contes de Fees* next.

Step 9: Use your *Peter Pan's Flight* Fastpass if it is time.

Step 10: Get a *Buzz Lightyear Laser Blast* Fastpass from Discoveryland.

Step 11: Have lunch.

Step 12: Ride *Pinocchio*, and *Snow White's Scary Adventures* in Fantasyland.

Step 13: Use your *Buzz Lightyear Laser Blast* Fastpass.

Step 14: Get a spot at least 45 minutes before the start of *Disney Stars on Parade* anywhere along the parade route. It is usually on at 5:30pm but make sure to check your Times Guide.

Step 15: Ride *Autopia* and/or explore inside *Sleeping Beauty Castle*. If there is a lot of time until park closing, do both. Fantasyland closes one hour before the other lands.

Step 16: Ride *"it's a small world"* in Fantasyland.

Step 17: Decision: *Explore Alice's Curious Labyrinth* or ride *Le Carousel de Lancelot*. If you still have a lot of time left until the park closes, do both.

Step 18: If any shows are playing, now is a great time to watch one.

Step 19: Ride *Pirates of the Caribbean* in Adventureland.

Step 20: Ride *Phantom Manor* in Frontierland.

Step 21: Have dinner and watch *Disney Illuminations*. Get a spot in front of the castle or on Main Street, U.S.A. at least 45 minutes before the show begins. See our section on *Disney Illuminations* to find the perfect spot.

Note: If your children want a thrill, *Big Thunder Mountain* in Frontierland should be your choice, as it does not go upside down and is the tamest roller coaster in the park.

1 Day without Extra Magic Hours - Focus: Thrills

Step 1: Arrive at 9:20am at the entrance to Disneyland Park. Enter as the park pre-opens at 9:30am. Until 10:00am you can shop and eat on Main Street, U.S.A. and ride the *Main Street Vehicles*. Pick up both a Park Guide and a Times Guide under the archways of *Main Street, U.S.A. Station*. These contain parade, show, character meeting and firework times, as well as attraction closures and park hours.

Step 2: Walk down Main Street, U.S.A., get photos and proceed straight to *Sleeping Beauty Castle*.

At Sleeping Beauty Castle's hub lies the entrance to all the lands of the park – Fantasyland and Discoveryland will be open to Disney Hotel guests and some Annual Pass Holders. Other lands will be cordoned off.

Stand by the rope leading to Frontierland. This rope is removed at 10:00am so all guests can go through.

Step 3: Ride *Big Thunder Mountain* in Frontierland immediately as the park opens.

Step 4: Ride *Star Wars Hyperspace Mountain* in Discoveryland.

Step 5: Ride *Star Tours*.

Step 6: Ride *Indiana Jones et le Temple du Peril* in Adventureland. Now you have ridden all the roller coasters in this park.

Step 7: Ride *Pirates of the Caribbean*.

Step 8: Get a *Buzz Lightyear Laser Blast* FastPass in Discoveryland.

Step 9: Time for lunch.

Step 10: Ride *Autopia*.

Step 11: If it is time for your *Buzz Lightyear Laser Blast* Fastpass, use it or skip to step 12.

Step 12: Ride *"it's a small world"*.

Step 13: Get a *Peter Pan's Flight* Fastpass.

Step 14: Use your *Buzz Lightyear Laser Blast* Fastpass if it still has not been used.

Step 15: Get a spot at least 45 minutes before the beginning of *Disney Stars on Parade* on Main Street, U.S.A. or anywhere else along the parade route.

Step 16: If you are interested in watching any shows, now is the perfect time.

Step 17: Ride *Phantom Manor*.

Step 18: Explore *Les Mystères de Nautilus* and other walkthroughs such as *Le Passage Enchanté d'Aladdin* or *La Cabane des Robinson*.

Step 19: Use your *Peter Pan's Flight* Fastpass and explore *Alice's Curious Labyrinth*.

Step 20: Have dinner.

Step 21: Get a spot in front of the Castle or on Main Street, U.S.A. at least 45 minutes before *Disney Illuminations*. See our section on *Disney Illuminations* for help finding the perfect spot.

---

2 Day Disneyland Park Touring Plan:
If you want to experience everything Disneyland Park has on offer in two days, follow the 1-Day plan for 'Kids Rides' on one day, followed by the 1-Day plan for 'Thrill Rides' the next day. This will cover all the rides in the most logical sequence. Combine the touring plans with Extra Magic Hours if you have those available to you and you should comfortably be able to experience Disneyland Park and all its attractions.

If you have three days or longer at Disneyland Park, there is no need to rigidly follow our touring plans. Make sure to arrive early, use Fastpass, and visit the busiest rides at the start or end of the day.

Walt Disney Studios Park

Step 1: Arrive at the Walt Disney Studios Park entrance by 9:20am. Enter the park at 9:30am when it pre-opens. Get a Park Map and a Times Guide as you enter *Studio 1*. Walk through *Studio 1* briskly and do not waste time looking around - you can do that later.

Step 2: When you come out of the other side of *Studio 1*, turn right after the statue of Mickey and Walt Disney and walk past *The Art of Disney Animation* and *Animagique Theater* towards the *Flying Carpets over Agrabah*.

To the left of *Flying Carpets over Agrabah* is *Crush's Coaster*. Form a queue outside the Wait Time sign or join the one that is already there. Ride *Crush's Coaster*.

Cast Member will usually start letting guests onto the ride just before 10:00.

Step 3: Pick up a Fastpass for *Ratatouille: The Adventure* as Fastpasses for this ride are distributed very quickly.

Step 4: Visit Toy Story Playland. There are several attractions to experience here. Ride them in this order: *Toy Soldiers Parachute Drop*, *RC Racer* and *Slinky Dog*.

Step 5: Ride *Cars Quatre Roues Rallye* – this is located opposite *Crush's Coaster*.

Step 6: Ride *Rock n' Roller Coaster*.

Step 7: Experience *Armageddon*.

Step 8: Hopefully at least two hours will have elapsed since you picked up your Fastpass for *Ratatouille: The Adventure*, so go and pick up a Fastpass for *The Twilight Zone: Tower of Terror*.

Step 9: Fit lunch in around your Fastpass time for *Ratatouille: The Adventure*. If it is time to ride the attraction now, do that first. If not, have lunch and return to use your Fastpass.

Step 10: Ride *Studio Tram Tour*. This attraction is in refurbishment from January to April 2017.

Step 11: Ride *Flying Carpets over Agrabah*.

Step 12: Use your *Tower of Terror* Fastpass if it is time. If it is not, then skip forward to step 13 and fit *Tower of Terror* in around the show times.

Step 13: That is it for all the rides. This park is tiny in comparison with Disneyland Park!

As well as the characters meets, there are five main shows left to experience, so take these in according to their schedules which are available in the Times Guide which you picked up earlier.

These shows are:
- *Lights, Motors, Action*
- *Stitch Live*
- *Disney Junior Live*
- *Mickey and The Magician*

Outside the Parks

A trip to Disneyland Paris does not have to stop at the resort. After all, you are near one of Europe's largest and most vibrant cities. In addition, there are opportunities for shopping and other adventures nearby.

Paris

Disneyland Paris is located a mere 35 minutes away from the centre of Paris by train, so visiting the 'City of Lights' is a must-do on an extended trip.

Paris is filled with monuments, museums, rich culture and history. You should make sure to visit some of the following world-class attractions during your time in the city: the Eiffel Tower, the *Louvre* museum, *Musée d'Orsay, Arc de Triomphe, Champs Elysées, Notre Dame, Montmartre* and the *Sacre Coeur.*

Museums are reasonably priced, and European Economic Area citizens aged under 26 get free entry to most museums in the city. In addition, non-EEA visitors under the age of 18 get free entry with proof. There are even monthly openings of the museums with free admission for everyone, regardless of age.

We recommend taking in a river cruise on The Seine or a bus tour, which will allow you to see several monuments in one go. Consider purchasing *The Independent Guide to Paris 2017* to plan your visit.

If you wish to visit several attractions and get unlimited public transport, the Paris Pass is worth considering.

To get to central Paris, catch the RER A train from *Marne-la-Vallee – Chessy* station, located just a two-minute walk from the parks. Once you are in the centre of Paris you may need to use the metro to get to various destinations.

A Mobilis day pass is the best travel ticket (priced at €16.60 for zones 1 to 5). It allows unlimited travel until midnight on Paris' transport system within Paris, and to and from Disneyland Paris.

Disneyland Paris sells two daily excursions to Paris:

Magical Day Tour of Paris – Coach transport with headsets detailing facts, history and culture in English. You will visit the second floor of the Eiffel Tower or the Louvre and cruise along the Seine and see the sights. Prices are £74 per adult and £49 per child. The bus departs from the Hotel New York at 9:45am and returns at approximately 6:30pm.

Paris Essentials – A free-style tour with time to explore alone. It includes a return coach trip from Disneyland Paris and a sightseeing bus tour in Paris. Prices are £47 per adult and £31 per child. The coach departs the Newport Bay Club Hotel, Magic Circus, and Hotel l'Elysée Val d'Europe from 10:15am to 10:40am. Returns at about 7:00pm.

Val d'Europe

Located just two minutes away from Disneyland Paris by train is *Val d'Europe* - a new town designed by Disney with a huge shopping centre.

It is only one stop away on the RER A line train (€1.90 per journey). Trains run every 10 minutes with a journey time of about 1 minute. Alternatively, you can catch the number 50 bus which is free from just outside *Marne la Vallée - Chessy* train station.

If you are taking the bus, you will exit at the last stop by the *Hotel l'Elysée*.

Cross the road at the pedestrian crossing and the shopping centre will be in front of you. These buses run somewhat infrequently during the day.

If using the RER train, make sure to leave *Val d'Europe* station through the exits marked *Centre Commercial*.

Outside the station, turn right and walk straight ahead, crossing the road. The shopping centre will be in front of you. Note that it is closed on some public holidays. Shops are open until 9:00pm from Monday to Saturday (and close at 8:00pm on Sunday), with restaurants staying open until about midnight daily.

If you would like to stock up on groceries, there is a hypermarket in the centre, as well as SeaLife aquarium (entry is €12 to €18 per person), and many other stores.

Follow the signs to *La Vallée Village* outlets for designer luxury goods at reduced prices.

Villages Nature (Opening in 2017)

Set to open in Summer 2017, *Villages Nature* is a partnership between Disneyland Paris and *Pierre et Vacances*. It is located 15 minutes from the main Disneyland Paris site.

This will be a new eco-tourism location built around a geothermal lagoon. There will be apartment-style accommodation available here and a shuttle bus will run to and from *Villages Nature* and Disneyland Paris.

There will be a variety of restaurants to enjoy, as well as recreation options.

The Aqualagoon will feature giant water slides, a wave pool, and an outdoor lagoon heated to 30°C year round.

Also on offer: BelleVie Farm will host educational programs and workshops; Extraordinary Gardens will be four landscaped gardens inspired by the Four Elements; Forest of Legends will be an outdoor playground; Treeclimbing trails; a bowling alley; boutiques; cultural events and much more. This all promises to be worth visiting.

Davy Crockett's Adventure

If you like adventure assault courses, you will love this! There are swings, trapezes, rope bridges, ladders and much more for you to explore, making this High Rope location great family fun.

This attraction is located at the entrance to Davy Crockett Ranch – a campsite run by Disneyland Paris and considered one of the seven on-site hotels. It is 8km from the main resort hub.

This activity is open seasonally – you should visit www.aventure-aventure.com (French only) for opening times (Under 'Pratique' and then 'Horaires'). The assault courses are operated by a third-party company and not Disneyland Paris.

Note there is no shuttle bus to the Davy Crockett Campsite where this activity is located, so you will need a car if you wish to participate in the experience, or alternatively you can book a taxi.

Golf Disneyland

Golf Disneyland is a world-class 27-hole golf course located right on Disneyland Paris property and open to all visitors, including hotel and day guests. You can rent out golf equipment and have a go yourself or watch others play.

Green fees for 18 holes start at about €50 per person on weekdays and €75 on weekends. 9 holes costs €35 and €45 respectively. A reduced rate for the 18-hole course is available for those aged under 25. The golf course is open year-round, except on Christmas Day and New Year's Day. Club rentals are €27 for a complete set, or €5 per club.

There is a restaurant and bar overlooking the course, and golf cart hire is available too.

The Pro Shop is also on site, which sells a large variety of golfing gear. Lessons are also available.

To make a reservation you can email dlp.golf.disneyland@disney.com or call +33 (0) 1 60 45 68 90.

Guests with Disabilities

Disneyland Paris is a place designed to be enjoyed by everyone, regardless of their mental or physical abilities. Over 60,000 disabled guests visit yearly.

Accessibility Cards

Parties of guests with disabilities should stop by Guest Relations at either park on the first day of their visit. In Disneyland Park this is City Hall (on the left after the train station) and at Walt Disney Studios Park this is at Studio Services (on the right before Studio 1).

At Guest Relations, guests who have a disability (permanent or temporary), and expectant mothers, can apply for one of two cards that will facilitate their visit: the Priority Card and the Easy Access Card.

The **Priority Card** allows a permanently disabled guest and up to 4 members of their party access to an attraction via a specially adapted entrance. This entrance will involve less walking and no stairs. It could be through the ride's exit, through the Fastpass entrance or through a specially adapted queue line. In cases that the standard queue line is adapted, you will use that one. Entry procedures vary from ride to ride – to learn the boarding options available to you at each attraction, ask a Cast Member at the ride entrances.

This card does not provide instant access; wait times vary based on the number of people in the Priority Card queue. In order to receive the card, the disabled person (or their helper) must present supporting documents or a medical certificate. Proof of ID is required and may be requested when boarding rides.

Supporting documentation to prove disability for guests from France includes one of the following: disability card, disabled person's priority card, difficulty standing card, war disability card or European disabled parking badge.

For guests from outside France, the following are accepted: disability card, European disabled parking badge or a medical certificate (stating the person has a disability in French or English, signed and stamped by a doctor and issued within the last 3 months).

The **Easy Access Card** is for guests with temporary or debilitating illnesses or injuries (that have not led to them being registered as disabled). The Easy

Access Card is also available for expectant mothers. It acts in the same way as the Priority Card, giving you access via a specially adapted entrance. This card does not officially offer priority access but the end result is similar to the Priority Card.

A medical certificate is required for this card. This certificate must state that the person has a debilitating illness, is temporary disabled or is pregnant in French or English, signed and stamped by a doctor and issued within the last 3 months. Only one helper may accompany the disabled guest on attractions, unless they have a *carte de priorité familiale* in which case all helpers named on the card may board with the disabled person.

Additional information: When a disabled person presents themselves at Guest Relations to ask for a Priority of Easy Access card, they are asked questions in order to determine their degree of handicap and which rides will be accessible to them. For example, someone who cannot transfer out of a wheelchair may not ride *Pirates of the Caribbean*.

As well as the card itself, you will be given a copy of the Accessibility Guide with detailed information on each attraction. You can also consult this in advance at www.bit.ly/dlpdisab before your trip.

Some attractions require that guests with Priority or Easy Access cards (and with certain disabilities) make a reservation at the ride entrance and return later. Character meet and greets usually work on a reservation system; there will be a Cast Member with characters to reserve a slot for you.

Some attractions may not be accessible to guests with certain disabilities. In this case, family members cannot use the card in place of the disabled person – they must use the standby queue or Fastpass, if available.

Certain disabilities may require that the disabled person be accompanied in order to ride.

Pregnant mothers may not ride certain attractions for their safety and will politely be refused access.

Accommodations for Disabled Guests

Hearing-impaired visitors: Disney Park information points, as well as some Walt Disney Studios Park attractions are equipped with induction loops to assist guests. These attractions are: *CinéMagique, Animagique Theatre, Disney Junior Live on Stage!, Stitch Live!* and *The Twilight Zone: Tower of Terror*.

Mobility impaired visitors: Cast Members cannot escort or help disabled guests to attractions. They will, of course, provide directions and assist inside attractions.

Some attractions require that disabled guests transfer from their wheelchair to an attraction vehicle. For these attractions, disabled guests must be accompanied by at least one able-bodied adult (18+) to assist. Cast Members may not help visitors in or out of their wheelchair or ride vehicles. For some attractions, visitors must be ambulatory.

In Walt Disney Studios Park, the queues for all attractions are wheelchair accessible; this is also the case for *Buzz Lightyear*

Laser Blast, Princess Pavilion and *Meet Mickey Mouse* in Disneyland Park. For attractions where this is not the case, a Priority Card allows guests entry via a separate entrance.

A designated viewing area for guests in wheelchairs is available for the parade, *Disney Illuminations* and shows.

All toilets have accessible areas for visitors with reduced mobility.

Unisex toilets (with cubicles so wheelchair users may be joined by a carer) are available in every land of Disneyland Park. They are also available at *Moteurs... Action ! Stunt Show Spectacular* in Walt Disney Studios Park during performances.

All shops and Table Service restaurants are accessible. At Quick Service places, ask a Cast Member for assistance if necessary.

An accessible shuttle bus is available between all Disney hotels (except Davy Crockett Ranch) and the theme parks. Simply ask at the hotel desk, the Disney Express desk in *Marne La Vallée – Chessy* station, or Guest Services in the parks for details and to book this free service.

Hotels each have rooms adapted to meet the needs of guests in wheelchairs. These have an extra-large bathroom with a bath, handrails and a raised toilet. Additionally, mobility-impaired guests can hire a seat to help them to wash without assistance (to be requested when making the reservation). The bedroom door has a spyhole at wheelchair height in accessible rooms. Bathrooms at Davy Crockett Ranch, Sequoia Lodge and Santa Fe Hotels have a shower suitable for mobility impaired guests.

Visually impaired guests:
At some attractions, a companion may need to describe the surroundings. Some attractions and areas of the park are dimly lit.

At hotels, Disney recommends that visually impaired guests inform the hotel reception of their visual impairment upon arrival. A Cast Member will show guests to their room, and show them around the rest of the Disney hotel so that visually impaired guests can orientate themselves. Telephones and television remotes with large buttons, as well as room keys with Braille, may be requested when making a reservation or at reception upon arrival.

Guide Dogs:
Guide and assistant dogs are allowed in the parks and on certain attractions. On attractions where they are not permitted, dogs must be left with a helper. Dogs may not be left unattended or with a Cast Member. Visually impaired guests may need to be accompanied on certain attractions. If bringing a guide dog, there must be at least two helpers with a disabled guest – one to accompany them, and another to take care of the guide dog whilst the others ride.

Food Allergies:
Disneyland Paris' food supplier offers allergen-free meals at selected restaurants. We recommend warning your hotel in advance so an allergen-free breakfast can be prepared. When booking Table Service meals, state your allergies. Review Disneyland Paris' allergen guide available at www.bit.ly/dlpallergy.

Other information:
Cast Members may refuse guests access to attractions for safety or other reasons.

Some attractions only accept one disabled guest at a time for safety and legal reasons. In these cases, the wait for a disabled guest can be as long or longer than the standard queue line.

Guests with medication that must be kept cool may leave it at one of the First Aid points in the two parks or in Disney Village.

For safety reasons, all visitors: with reduced mobility or visual impairment, with a cognitive or mental health disorder, with behaviour disorder or autism or with a learning disability, must be accompanied by at least one able-bodied companion over the age of 18 to assist them. Some attractions allow helpers to accompany several people with disabilities (details are in the Disney Accessibility Guide).

Some attractions may have low-light areas, flashing lights or loud sound effects, dropping floors and other effects. Companions should pay particular attention to all these factors when preparing for the stay and should read the safety information available at the entrance to each attraction, as well as the Disney Parks Accessibility Guide.

Meeting The Characters

For many visitors of all ages, meeting their favourite Disney characters is the highlight of a trip to Disneyland Paris. Being able to play games with Pluto, talk to Cinderella and hug Mickey always makes for magical moments that last forever.

Disneyland Park:
Characters are scheduled to appear around the park at different times throughout the day.

Mickey can be found in his "backstage" theatre area at *Meet Mickey Mouse* in Fantasyland, and the Disney princesses can be found at *Princess Pavilion* (also in Fantasyland).

Near *Alice's Curious Labyrinth* you will find Alice and her friends, including The Mad Hatter and Tweedle Dum and Dee. Also nearby, you can meet Winnie the Pooh and Friends.

By Plaza Gardens you can see Donald and friends, whereas there are usually other characters by Casey's Corner on Main Street, U.S.A. By the

Liberty Arcade, you can find Minnie and friends.

Woody and Friends are by Cowboy Cookout Restaurant, and Chip and Dale can be found by Hakuna Matata Restaurant in Adventureland.

Elsewhere in Adventureland, you can expect to see Peter Pan and friends by *Pirate's Beach*, and Aladdin and friends near Agrabah Café.

When *Star Tours* re-opens in March 2017, there will also be a Star Wars meet and greet location opposite the ride entrance.

If there is a specific character you would like to see, ask at City Hall (on Town Square) whether they have a non-public

schedule for them. Not all characters are available to meet on all days, especially the more minor ones.

You can also have a Disney princess dining experience at *L'Auberge de Cendrillon* (priced at €75 per adult, €45 per child).

Starting in late March 2017, you will also be able to meet Disney characters at Plaza Gardens on Main Street, U.S.A for breakfast.

Walt Disney Studios Park:
You will find many characters in the Toon Studio area of the park to the left of *Crush's Coaster* at permanent outdoor photo locations. Here you will often find Mickey, Minnie, Buzz Lightyear, Woody and other characters. Check your Times Guide for exact character appearances.

Guests also have the opportunity to meet and greet Spider-Man himself at *Meet Spider-Man*, located just opposite the entrance to *Rock 'n' Roller Coaster* at Walt Disney Studios Park. Other Marvel characters may replace Spider-Man at this location in the future.

For a limited time starting in November 2016, you will also be able to meet Moana in *Art of Disney Animation*.

Hotels:
Characters are present in the on-site hotel lobby in the morning.

Classic characters such as Mickey, Minnie, Tigger, Chip and Dale and Donald Duck are also present during the character meals at Inventions restaurant in

Disneyland Hotel. Lunch and Dinner meals are priced at €65 adults, and €35 for kids. Inventions also hosts a themed brunch on Sundays priced at €70 adults, €35 kids, from 1:00pm to 3:00pm – you can take part in both even if you are not staying here.

Disney Village:
You can meet the characters in Disney Village at Cafe Mickey and Buffalo Bill's Wild West Show.

Cafe Mickey serves breakfast, lunch and dinner; characters rotate often but feature the classics like Mickey Mouse, Pluto, Chip and Dale, Goofy and Minnie. Specific characters cannot be guaranteed as they change regularly. We expect this location to close in late March 2017.

At *Buffalo Bill's Wild West Show* you can get a photo with Mickey Mouse in his Wild West costume before the show. Be there early as Mickey heads off early to prepare for the show. Admission into the show is required. Other characters participate in the show but are not available to meet.

CHARACTER MEETING TIPS:

• *Meet Mickey Mouse* and *Princess Pavilion* have full queuing areas with a wait time posted by the entrance. Most other characters in the Times Guide have a queue formed with the help of Cast Members; you can expect a wait of about one minute per group ahead of you – some will spend longer with the characters, but most will average around one minute.

• Unscheduled character meets have no queue at all. Guests crowd around the character and you simply have to nudge forward to get a turn.

• People of all ages get photos and autographs with characters, not just young children.

• Most characters have a character helper. You can ask them to take a photo of you with your camera if you would like.

• Never injure a character, or pull on them or their costume.

• Characters stay in role at all times – interact with them and ask them about something from their film.

• Some characters are silent – all 'fur' characters where you cannot see a performer's human face cannot talk.

Doing Disney on a Budget

A visit to Disneyland Paris is expensive – it is a premium theme park destination and with travel, park tickets, accommodation, food and souvenirs it is easy to see why many families save up for a long time for a visit. However, there are many ways of reducing your spending at the resort yet still have a magical time.

Travel

Driving – Most visitors from Europe can simply drive to the resort. For example, if going from the south-east of England to Disneyland Paris, driving can be a good option.

You will need to purchase a ferry crossing or travel through the Eurotunnel (£50-£150 return when booked in advance) for a car and all its passengers crossing from the UK to France.

From Calais, in France, is it an easy three-hour drive. There are about €18 of tolls each way from Calais to Disneyland Paris, plus petrol costs.

Budget flights – Flights are available from £20/€30 each way from across Europe to Paris. *Charles de Gaulle* airport is the most convenient, followed by *Orly*. Be wary of *Paris Beauvais-Tille* Airport, which is actually 120km away from Disneyland Paris.

Train – Finally, there are TGV and Eurostar trains to get you to the resort. If travelling across France, take a look at Ouigo (www. ouigo.com), which offers cheap travel on TGV trains from locations across France.

On the TGV, 'Prems' fares booked in advance can also be good value. You will arrive at *Marne la Vallée – Chessy* station.

For UK visitors, Eurostar trains start at £72 return if booked in advance.

Those from the regions can book "through fares" from their home station to Disneyland Paris through the Eurostar website, changing trains at St. Pancras. For example, Manchester to Paris starts at £90 return.

With trains, you do not need airport transfers, so factor that into your price comparisons.

Planning

1. Hotels – Do you need a Disney hotel? They are themed but are also very expensive compared to other hotels. Nearby hotels, such as the Kyriad, have offers from €60 per night. However, a non-Disney hotel means no Extra Magic Hours, and separate park tickets.

Alternatively, stay at a cheaper Disney hotel such as the Hotel Cheyenne or Santa Fe to get the on-site benefits.

2. Buy an annual pass – If you are visiting for at least three days, an annual pass can work out cheaper than a three-day ticket and you get dining and merchandise discounts. It is even better value if you do two trips within a year.

3. Use a special offer – There is always a special offer running, whether it is 'kids go free', or an extra day and night free. Do not book without an offer. If there are no offers, wait a few days.

4. Tickets – If you are not staying at a Disney hotel, pre-purchase your tickets. Buying them at the ticket booths on the day is expensive and a waste of time.

5. Visit off-peak – The parks are less busy, you can do more each day and hotels are cheaper.

At the Parks

1. Eat in Disney Village – It is not the healthiest option, but the McDonald's in Disney Village sells fast-food at prices much cheaper than food in the theme parks. Or try, the well-priced Earl of Sandwich next door. Vapiano also offers a well-priced, tasty Italian meal.

2. Meal vouchers – If you want to eat at restaurants every day of your stay, then pre-purchasing meal vouchers online or over the phone can save you money. They can be added when booking or any time before your trip if you are staying at a Disney hotel. Vouchers must be purchased for the entire stay.

3. Packed lunches – Make your own packed lunches or save a few croissants from breakfast at your hotel (an ethically grey area). There is also a mini-market at *Marne-La-Vallee - Chessy* train station called Casino that stocks essentials that you can take into the parks with you. There is also a huge supermarket called Auchan in *Val d'Europe*. Alternatively, bring food and snacks from home.

4. Take your own photos – If you do not want to pay €15 for a character photo, take one yourself; the Cast Members do not mind. They will even take the photo for you if you ask.

5. Combine photos – Paying €15 for a single on-ride photo is expensive, as are character photos. See our section on Disneyland Paris' Photopass and Photopass+ services for unlimited photos for a set price.

6. Take your own merchandise – Buy dresses, outfits and toys outside of Disneyland Paris. Get these from Disney Stores, online or at supermarkets before you leave for Disneyland Paris. Give your child the costume once you arrive and they will be over the moon. This saves paying the inflated in-park merchandise prices.

7. More affordable meals – Although food prices are expensive, there are some better value restaurants than others. Also, try the set menus with a main course, dessert and drink for one price. Or, try a buffet as a late lunch and have snacks at dinner.

Dining

There are a wide variety of places to eat at Disneyland Paris. Food options vary from sandwich and snack locations, to Quick Service (fast food) places, character buffets, Table Service dining and even fine dining options. Eating is as much of the experience as the attractions.

Making Reservations

If you want to guarantee you will be able to dine at a specific restaurant, it is worth booking advance.

You can make your restaurant reservation up to 60 days in advance, but in reality booking even two weeks or less beforehand will usually get you a table at most places.

Most people do not book restaurants in theme parks in Europe far in advance, which is a stark change from the American Disney parks.

Despite this, it is worth making a reservation as early as possible if you want a specific meal on a specific day. You will also be seated much more quickly with a reservation than without one.

Purchasing a meal plan does not guarantee you a table in a restaurant, so be sure to make a restaurant reservation in advance if there is a particular place you want to dine.

You can call the Dining Reservation hotline on +33 (0)1 60 30 40 50 and book in several languages, including English. You can also book at City Hall in Disneyland Park, Studio Services in Walt Disney Studios or at any of the Disney hotel lobbies. In addition, you can visit any of the restaurants and book directly.

You do not need to be staying in a Disney hotel to book a table at a restaurant. If you cannot attend a reservation, it is good practice to cancel it as soon as possible.

In low season, we have often walked into restaurants on the day and got reservations for the same day or the next day. In the high season, restaurants are fully booked a week or more in advance.

Top Tip: If you wish to dine at Auberge de Cendrillon, specifically, it is worth booking well in advance.

Meal Plans

Meal Plans allow you to pre-purchase meal credits, so that on arrival at the resort, you do not need to worry about the cost of meals. Meal Plans are available to guests who book packages with a hotel and park tickets.

A meal voucher includes a set menu or buffet, plus one soft drink.

Occasionally, Disneyland Paris runs a promotion with a free Meal Plan with package bookings.

Meal Plans are paper vouchers given at check-in. Simply hand them over when it is time to pay for your meal. This paper system is being phased out and you may get a Magic Card that stores meal vouchers digitally instead.

There are four different Meal Plans to choose from. More expensive Meal Plans include higher quality restaurants and food items.

Not every restaurant accepts every Meal Plan; if you eat at a restaurant not included on your Meal Plan, you can use your vouchers for a discount. E.g. If you a have 'Plus' voucher, but visit a 'Premium' restaurant, the 'Plus' voucher's value will be deducted from your bill, and you pay the difference.

Vouchers can be used at most Quick Service locations. We do not recommend this as the vouchers are worth more than a Quick Service meal so you would be wasting them. The exception to this is the Hotel Meal Plan.

Meal Plans can save you up to 15% off the meal prices; this varies based on what you eat. For many guests, the piece of mind of pre-paid meals is the best part.

Pricing:
When booking, you can either choose a Half Board option for one meal per day, or a Full Board option for two meals per day. Prices are at the bottom of this page and include breakfast, which is an extra charge for non-meal plan guests.

As well as the two standard meals per day, guests who buy the Standard, Plus or Premium Meal Plans get a free *Pause Gourmande* (teatime drink and treat).

Hotel Meal Plan prices listed vary - the better the hotel you stay in, the more the meal plan costs.

Meals are from a set menu on the "Standard" and "Plus" plans. On the Premium Plan you can order 'a la carte'. If in doubt, show your vouchers to your waiter before ordering.

For Hotel Meal Plans only: Half Board plans include one dinner buffet voucher at your hotel's restaurant. Full Board plans include one dinner buffet voucher at your hotel's restaurant plus a lunch voucher for a meal at one Quick Service location in the parks. Breakfast is also included.

For all other Meal Plans: The Half Board plan includes one voucher for any restaurant from the grid on the next page; the Full Board plan includes two vouchers for restaurants of your choice from the grid. Breakfast is also included.

	Hotel Adult	Hotel Child	Standard Adult	Standard Child	Plus Adult	Plus Child	Premium Adult	Premium Child
Half Board	From £25	From £18	£27	£19	£38	£25	£62	£42
Full Board	From £34	From £23	£42	£28	£53	£34	£88	£56

Restaurant Name	Restaurant Type	Location	On Hotel Plan?	On Standard Plan?	On Plus Plan?	On Premium Plan?
Agrabah Cafe	Buffet	Disneyland Park	No	Yes	Yes	Yes
Annette's Diner	Table Service	Disney Village	No	No	Yes	Yes
Auberge de Cendrillon	Table Service	Disneyland Park	No	No	No	Yes
Beaver Creek Tavern	Table Service	Sequoia Lodge Hotel	No	No	Yes	Yes
Bistrot Chez Remy	Table Service	Walt Disney Studios Park	No	No	Yes	Yes
Blue Lagoon	Table Service	Disneyland Park	No	No	Yes	Yes
Buffalo Bill's Wild West Show	Table Service Show	Disney Village	No	No	No	Yes
Cafe Mickey	Table Service Character	Disney Village	No	No	Yes	Yes
California Grill	Table Service	Disneyland Hotel	No	No	No	Yes
Cape Cod	Buffet	Newport Bay Club Hotel	Yes	No	Yes	Yes
Chuck Wagon Cafe	Buffet	Hotel Cheyenne	Yes	Yes	Yes	Yes
Crockett's Tavern	Buffet	Davy Crockett's Ranch	Yes	Yes	Yes	Yes
Hunter's Grill	Buffet	Sequoia Lodge Hotel	Yes	No	Yes	Yes
Inventions	Character Buffet	Disneyland Hotel	Yes	No	No	Yes
La Cantina	Buffet	Santa Fe Hotel	Yes	Yes	Yes	Yes
La Grange at Billy Bob's	Table Service	Disney Village	No	Yes	Yes	Yes
Manhattan Restaurant	Table Service	Hotel New York	No	No	Yes	Yes
Plaza Gardens	Buffet	Disneyland Park	No	Yes	Yes	Yes
Parkside Diner	Buffet	Hotel New York	Yes	No	Yes	Yes
Restaurant des Stars	Buffet	Walt Disney Studios Park	No	Yes	Yes	Yes
Silver Spur Steakhouse	Table Service	Disneyland Park	No	No	Yes	Yes
The Steakhouse	Table Service	Disney Village	No	No	Yes	Yes
Walt's: An American Restaurant	Table Service	Disneyland Park	No	No	No	Yes

Tipping in Restaurants

In France, a 15% service charge is included in your meal price, although this may not be itemised in the bill.

You are not expected to leave any additional money for service.

If you particularly liked the service, free to leave a few Euros in cash as a tip. A 5% to 10% tip is more than enough, though it is rare to see a French person tip.

Sometimes in France, waiters will not return with your change and will assume it is their tip; if this was not your intention, make this known. This is much less common at Disneyland Paris than elsewhere. One way to avoid this is to always pay by card.

Good to Know

• For buffets, kids' prices apply for those aged 3 to 11 years of age.

• Until late March 2017, a breakfast buffet is included every morning of your stay at Disney hotels. You have the option of having breakfast in the parks or in the Disney Village for an extra fee. Ask at reception for the availability of these experiences.

• Adults can generally order from the kids' menu, especially at Quick Service locations.

• For an idea of how much food costs at the restaurants, check out the parks chapters which list set menu prices and a la carte main courses, as well as some individual items.

• Not all restaurants have a vegan or vegetarian option, but Cast Members and chefs will do their best to accommodate you. Making a reservation and starting your dietary requirements helps.

Breakfast Pricing

From 29th March 2017, breakfast will no longer be included in Disney packages. Unless you get a meal plan, you will need to pay for breakfast separately.

These are the prices per person per night for breakfast.

• **Davy Crockett Ranch** - €10 adult or child
• **Santa Fe and Cheyenne** - €16 per adult, €14 per child
• **Sequoia Lodge** - €19 per adult, €17 per child
• **Newport Bay Club and Hotel New York** - €25 per adult, €23 per child
• **Disneyland Hotel** - €30 per adult, €27 per child

RESTAURANT TYPES:

Buffet – All-you-can-eat locations where you fill up your plate from the food selection as many times as you want. Buffets may or may not include drinks.

Quick Service – Fast food. Look at the menus above the cashiers, pay for your food and collect it a few minutes later. You will find everything from burgers and chips, to chicken, to pizza and pasta. Be aware that Disney 'fast'-food locations are notoriously slow and a queue of just four or five people in front of you can easily be a wait time of 20 to 30 minutes.

Table Service – Where you order from a menu, and are served by a waiter who brings your food to your table.

Character Buffets – These are available all day and are all-you-can eat places where characters interact with you and take photos as you eat.

Top Tip: Whether it be a snack cart, a Quick Service location or a Table Service restaurant, you are never obliged to order from a set menu. Ordering specific items 'a la carte' is completely fine, although it may save you money if you order certain set menu combinations.

Useful to Know

We have taken a look at the theme parks, hotels, Disney Village and even outside the resort so far, but there is still much more to cover.

When to Visit

Crowds at Disneyland Paris vary greatly from season to season, and even day to day. The difference of a single day can save you hundreds on accommodation and hours in queues.

You need to consider national and school holidays in France and surrounding countries, the weather, pricing and more to find the best time to go. Here is a detailed guide of the best times to visit Disneyland Paris, even including a detailed analysis of weekdays.

MAJOR HOLIDAYS (TIMES TO AVOID):

Late 2016
• 16th December to 31st December: Christmas Break. 31 Dec is very busy.

In 2017
• 1st to 3rd January: New Year's Day & School Break
• 17th February to 5th March: French and UK school break
• 17th March: St. Patrick's Day (extra celebrations including fireworks means slightly larger crowds)
• 31st March to 2nd May: Easter Holidays - Particularly busy from 14th April to 1st May.
• 6th to 8th May: Victory in Europe Day weekend

• 25th May to 28th May: Ascension Day weekend
• 2nd June to 5th June: Pentecost/Whit Sunday
• 15th June to 10th September: European School Summer Break. August is by far the busiest month. July is busier than June. September is less busy from the 4th onwards.
• 14th July: Bastille Day (Bank Holiday)
• 15th August: Assumption of Mary
• Weekends in September: Extremely busy.
• October weekends: Very busy as Parisians see the Halloween festivities.
• 19th October to 5th

November: UK and France School Holidays and Halloween
• 22nd December 2017 to 7th January 2018 - Christmas Holidays. 31st Dec is the busiest day.

Top Tip: If a public holiday falls on a Friday or a Monday, that weekend becomes a *pont* (a long weekend). If it is on a Thursday or Tuesday, many people turn this into a 4-day weekend. You should avoid *ponts* at all costs as there are weekend crowds from Paris, plus the visitors from the rest of France making it very busy.

BEST TIMES TO VISIT:

• January: Excluding the first four or five days, when there are still school holidays on. In general, this is a good time to visit. Crowds are non-existent. The weather is very cold.

• First half of February: The weather is freezing but the parks are a ghost town. This is the slowest period of the year with very low visitor numbers.

• Second half of March to: Low crowds, but cold.

• May: Excluding bank holidays. At this time of the year, the weather is improving but it is certainly not T-shirt and shorts weather.

• The first two weeks of June: Starting to get warmer, and with low crowds before the school holidays. Avoid Whit Sunday weekend. Mid-June onwards starts to get busier.

• Mid-September to mid-October: Kids are back at school and the weather is quite nice. This is perhaps the best time to visit. Plus, in October you have Halloween entertainment. Avoid weekends, which are very busy.

•The week between the Halloween and Christmas seasons: Except when a school holiday takes place during this week. This is one of the slowest weeks of the year and is comparable to February in terms of visitor numbers. The park is "normal", with no Halloween or Christmas entertainment.

• The second week of November until mid-December: Cold but low crowds. Going during this time of the year also means you will get all the Christmas decorations and entertainment. November is a very off-peak time.

DAYS OF THE WEEK:

The days of the week that you visit make a large difference to the time it takes to get you onto rides. A ride can have a wait time of 90 minutes on one day, and just 30 minutes or less the next. The most notable difference is between weekends and weekdays.

The best day of the week to visit is Monday, followed by Tuesday, then Thursday, then Wednesday, Friday, Sunday, and finally the busiest day of the week is by far Saturday. Park hours are often extended on weekends to compensate for the larger crowds.

Parking

Many guests drive to Disneyland Paris, as it is a practical and affordable way to travel. If you will be doing this, simply follow the signs to theme park parking when you are near the resort.

Parking is charged for all guests, except some Annual Passholders and Disney hotel guests. The price is €20 per car, €35 for a caravan and €15 for a motorbike.

From the parking area to the theme parks is a 10 to 15-minute walk including the use of travelators. Guests staying at on-site

Disney hotels get a free shuttle service to the park, but can also opt to drive to the theme parks instead and get complimentary parking by showing their Magic Card or Easy Pass at the parking payment booths. You will not save any time driving instead of using the hotel shuttles, as the routes are so short.

Disney Village also has its own multi-story *Indigo* car park a 2-minute walk from the theme parks – significantly closer than the theme park parking. It is €24 for a day, instead of €20 but it is usually much less busy than the main car park. There is no free parking here for Disney hotel guests or annual pass holders.

Disneyland Paris App

Disneyland Paris has a free Apple iOS and Android app, which allows you to enhance your trip. With the app, you can plan your stay including an overview of the hotels on offer, and a look at the different attractions throughout the resort. You can even create an itinerary.

Once in the park, you can check the opening hours, timings of shows and parades, and even the attraction wait times. It is this last feature that makes the app the most useful – no more walking to the wait time board on Main Street, U.S.A. You can just check waits in the palm of your hand for both parks at the same time.

You will need a data connection to see live information, which means you must have data roaming enabled on your phone.

Data usage is minimal for the app, but it may cost you depending on your roaming agreement if you are not from France. Roaming charges in the EU will be abolished on 15th June 2017 under current plans.

Disneyland Paris plans to have free Wi-Fi available in both parks by early 2017.

On-Ride Photos

Some of Disneyland Paris' rides have cameras positioned and timed to take perfect on-ride photos of you at the most action filled moments on attractions. Buy the photo and see yourself at the fastest, steepest, scariest and most fun moment of the ride. These make for timeless keepsakes.

When you get off a ride, you will walk past screens that show you a preview of your photo (with a watermark on top). If you wish to purchase it, simply go to the photo counter.

You do not have to buy on-ride photos straight after your ride; you can pick them up at any time that same day. Just remember your unique number at the ride exit or ask a member of staff at the photo kiosk to write it down for you.

If you like the photo, Cast Members will show it to you up close before you pay for it. If you like it, buy it! It is something you will treasure for a long time.

Photo print prices are €16 for one photo, €21 for two photos and €26 for three photos. Digital photos are also available via the Photopass+ app – more details on the following pages.

The attractions with on-ride photos are: *Big Thunder Mountain*, *Pirates of the Caribbean*, *Star Wars Hyperspace Mountain*, *Buzz Lightyear Laser Blast*, *Rock n' Roller

Coaster*, and *The Twilight Zone: Tower of Terror*.

Top Tip: If you want photos from several rides, you can combine these together on a Photopass. See our next section on Photopass to find out how to save money on photos.

Photopass

Disneyland Paris' Photopass is an easy to use system that makes collecting all your in-park photos easy.

Simply go to any in-park photographer (including those stationed at *Meet Mickey Mouse*, *Princess Pavilion*, and other characters) and after your photo is taken, ask for a Disney Photopass.

Alternatively, you can ask for a Photopass card at any ride photo counter (this option is not advertised but is available if you ask).

This card can then be re-used throughout both parks anywhere you find a photographer or with on-ride photos. Simply hand over your card and photos throughout your visit will be added onto it and all kept together on the system.

Photos are saved on the Photopass system for 7 days each. For annual Passholders, photos can be saved onto your annual pass and will expire after 90 days.

Before your photos expire, visit one of these locations to view and purchase your photos: *New Century Notions: Flora's Unique Boutique* in Disneyland

Park, *Walt Disney Studios Store* in Walt Disney Studios Park, and T*he Disney Gallery* in Disney Village. Photos can also be viewed at the Disney shops inside the on-site hotels.

At all these locations, you can purchase prints and/or digital versions of your Photopass photos.

If you amass multiple Photopass cards, they can be combined into one account when purchasing your photos too.

Pricing for photos is as follows: €16 for 1 photo, €21 for 2 photos, €26 for 3 photos, €31 for 4 photos, subsequent photos cost €5 each. Each print can be different or you can get multiples of the same photo – it is up to you.

The more photos you purchase, the lower the overall 'price per photo'

becomes.

You can add also an extra element of Disney magic with themed borders and details at no additional cost.

For those who have used the Photopass system in the US parks, the Disneyland Paris system works in a similar manner, but the prints are generally more reasonably priced at Disneyland Paris.

The biggest difference, however, is the lack of Photopass photographers throughout the parks in France whereas there are several of them in each park in the US, allowing you to get great photos with the parks' icons. This is one by the castle but we hope this is expanded throughout the park in the future.

Photopass+

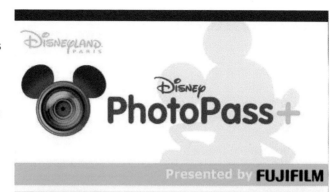

Like the regular Photopass (covered on the previous page), Photopass+ allows you to collect ride and character photos. The difference here is that you pre-pay for an unlimited number of digital photos instead of paying for each print individually. Photopass+ is priced at €59,99.

Guests who purchase Photopass+ get a Photopass+ card and a lanyard to carry the card around on. In addition, two mini cards are also included, so that other members of your party can have their own card and easily add photos to the same account.

This allows, for example, a mum to ride *Big Thunder Mountain* with the kids and add on-ride photos to the account at the same time that Dad rides *Star Wars Hyperspace Mountain* and adds his on-ride photo to the same account.

Guests can add an unlimited number of photos to their account for up to 10 days following their Photopass+ activation.

To view photos, guests should create an online account at www.disneyphotopass.eu or

via the iOS and Android 'Disneyland Paris Photopass' mobile apps.

With the mobile app, after riding an attraction you can simply scan the QR code on the ride photo preview monitors and have it added to your account without the need to visit the ride photo counters. Guests can also type in the photo number as it appears on these photo preview screens.

Guests can view their photos on the DisneyPhotopass.eu website and download them in high quality, as well as buy prints, photo books, calendars, gifts and more.

Photos stay on the Photopass+ website for one year after they were taken, giving you plenty of time to download your favourite photos.

Photopass+ at Disneyland Paris is very similar to the system in the US parks – but on a smaller scale.

Guests who pre-book Photopass+ as part of their stay get a €10 discount. A Photopass+ voucher will be given at check-in that must be exchanged for the actual product at any shop in the parks that sells Photopass+.

Top Tip: Annual Pass discounts are available. Annual pass holders also get a Photopass+ card valid for one year from the date of purchase instead of just 10 days, offering fantastic value for money.

Top Tip 2: If you have not bought Photopass+, you can also buy individual digital photos on the Photopass app. These are £2.99/€3,59 each, or £7.99/€9,99 for six.

Rider Switch

Rider Switch (also known as Baby Switch) is a time-saving solution that allows parents to reduce queuing times throughout their visit when riding thrill attractions.

A common issue at theme parks is when two adults want to ride a roller coaster, but they have a child who is not tall enough to ride. There are three solutions: a) the adults can take turns to ride (queuing twice), b) one adult can choose not to experience the attraction, c) forego the attraction altogether. The solution? Disney's Rider Switch service.

Rider Switch allows one adult to queue up and ride while the other stays with the child. When the first adult reaches the end of the queue line they can ask for a Rider Switch pass. The second adult is then able to ride as soon as the first one returns to take care of the child – the second adult is granted almost immediate access to the ride, usually through the exit, bypassing the entire regular queue line. Each adult will experience the ride separately but the second adult will not need to queue up.

The system varies from attraction to attraction so make sure to ask a Cast Member at the entrance how the system works with that particular ride.

This system is often called Baby Switch but is officially named Rider Switch. You do not necessarily have to have a child or baby present to use this service. You could use it to stay with someone who is scared or unable to ride. Whether you call it Baby Switch, or Rider Switch, the principles are the same.

Single Rider

One of the best ways to significantly reduce your time waiting in queues is to use the Single Rider queue instead of the regular standby queue. This is available at selected attractions at the resort.

A Single Rider queue is used to fill free spaces on ride vehicles. For example, if a ride vehicle can seat 8 people and a group of 4 turns up, followed by a group of 3, then a single rider will be put onto the ride from the Single Rider queue line.

This fills up the empty space on the ride vehicle, whilst also allowing guests who are willing to ride with strangers to wait for significantly shorter amount of time. Ultimately this system reduces wait times for everyone.

When the theme parks get extremely busy, Single Rider lines may be temporarily closed if the wait in the Single Rider queue is the same or greater than the standby line. If the theme parks are not very busy, then Single Rider Lines may not operate as they are not necessary.

Single Rider Lines can be used for by groups too, not just individuals but members of the group will be separated and each will ride in a different vehicle. You can, of course, wait for each other after riding by the exit.

Selected attractions operate Single Rider Lines. The following attractions have this system in operation:

• *RC Racer*
• *Toy Soldier Parachute Drop*
• *Crush's Coaster*
• *Ratatouille: The Adventure*
• *Star Wars Hyperspace Mountain*

Disneyland Paris has announced that it wishes to increase the number of Single Rider lines at the parks, so you can expect the selection to increase in the future.

Extra Magic Hours

Extra Magic Hours (EMH) allow selected guests up to two hours of early theme park access to selected attractions at Disneyland Paris each morning. Guests get access to an almost empty park, ride with little to no wait and can meet Disney characters.

EMHs usually take place at Disneyland Park from 8:00am to 10:00am. At selected times of the year, this is reduced to 1 hour or 1 hour and 30 minutes. EMHs are offered daily.

EMHs are also offered at Walt Disney Studios Park instead of Disneyland Park for 2 hours per day on selected dates. During very busy periods, EMHs may be offered at both parks. Check the Disneyland Paris website for details.

Getting Extra Magic Hours
The EMHs benefit is available exclusively to guests staying at on-site Disney Hotels (not selected or partner hotel) and for guests who have a *Magic Plus* or *Infinity* Annual Passport, even if they are not staying at a Disney hotel.

Disney hotel guests will need their park tickets and their Magic Card or Easy Pass (given at hotel check-in) to gain entry during Extra Magic Hours. Annual pass holders just need their annual pass to get in. Magic Plus Annual Pass holders cannot enter during EMHs on blackout dates.

What is open during EMHs
At Disneyland Park selected attractions on Main Street, U.S.A., and in Fantasyland and Discoveryland.

Disneyland Paris does not publish a list of the rides that operate during this period. Typically, the following rides are available during Extra Magic Hours – other rides and lands open at the official park opening time:
• Fantasyland – *Dumbo: The Flying Elephant, Peter Pan's Flight, The Adventures of Pinocchio, Lancelot's Carousel* and *Mad Hatter's Teacups*.
• Discoveryland – *Star Wars Hyperspace Mountain, Buzz Lightyear Laser Blast* and *Orbitron*.

Extra Magic Hours at Walt Disney Studios Park are rare and only happen a few weeks each year. In the past the following attractions have operated during Studios EMHs: *The Twilight Zone: Tower of Terror, Rock n' Roller Coaster, Crush's Coaster, Cars: Quatre Roues Rallye, Ratatouille: The Adventure, Toy Soldiers Parachute Drop, Slinky Dog Zigzag Spin* and *RC Racer*.

In our opinion, the Extra Magic Hours at the Studios offer more time savings than at Disneyland Park overall as there are more major attractions open, especially for thrill seekers.

Larger Guests

Disneyland Paris has designed its attractions to be able to be ridden by all guests, but sometimes a visitor's height or weight may limit the attractions they can visit for safety reasons.

At Disneyland Paris, unlike many other theme parks, there are no 'test seats' outside attractions. Therefore, if you are unsure whether you will be able to ride a certain attraction, it is best to speak to a Cast Member at the ride entrance.

You could also ask the Cast Member whether they could allow you to try sitting in the ride vehicle itself before queuing up normally.

Rides where larger guests may have difficulty include: *Rock 'n' Roller Coaster, Star Wars Hyperspace Mountain, Indiana Jones et le Temple du Peril, Crush's Coaster* and *RC Racer* because of the restraints and limited legroom.

Orbitron and *Cars Quatre Roues Rallye* can also be a tight fit despite using seatbelt-style restraints.

Guided Tours

If you want to discover more about the magic behind Disneyland Paris' two theme parks be sure to take part in one of the guided tours the resort offers. Led by a member of Guest Relations, these tours are the perfect way to enhance your visit.

The Disneyland Park tour departs at 1:00pm or 2:00pm each day, and the Walt Disney Studios Park tour departs at 3:00pm daily.

Each tour lasts two hours and you will discover the work that goes into creating these parks. You will find out secrets and notice details that will make you stop and say "WOW".

The tour is available in any of the six official park languages, including English.

Additionally, *The Twilight Zone: Tower of Terror* tour goes into the details of the construction and design of The Hollywood Tower Hotel, as well as the references from *The Twilight Zone* TV series. Your tour will conclude with a ride on the attraction, if you dare. Tours are held in French only at 9:10am on Wednesdays and Saturdays. This is before the park officially opens, meaning you can experience an empty park too.

Pricing for the park tours is €50 per adult and €30 for children ages 3 to 11 inclusive. The *Tower of Terror* tour is €40 per adult and €24 per child.

Reservations can be made by emailing Disney Special Activities at dlp.disney. special.activities@disney. com.

Disney Shopping Service

The Disney Shopping Service allows you to purchase any item at any of the theme park shops and not have to carry it around with you all day.

When paying for your goods before 3:00pm, simply ask to use the Disney Shopping Service.

You will fill in some details and leave the item with the Cast Member who served you. When you have finished your day at the park, you can pick up your item.

The item will not be available at the exact shop you purchased it from. Instead, to make things easy, you can then either pick up your purchases at the World of Disney store in Disney Village in the evening, or at the Disney boutiques at your on-site Disney hotel or at selected partner hotels.

This means that if you have multiple items from multiple shops, you can collect them all in one place.

This is a great service that allows you to be free to eat, shop, ride attractions and watch shows to your heart's content without having to worry about carrying any bags.

Speaking French

All Cast Members at the resort speak French. Most Cast Members at the resort also speak English.

Therefore, for the most part, the language barrier is not a problem when talking to Cast Members.

However, knowing the basics in French is really helpful, and employees do appreciate it if you say *Bonjour* and then switch to English, or even better say *Parlez-vous Anglais?* [*pronounced par-lay-voo-zarn-glay*] for "Do you speak English?".

You may occasionally come across a Cast Member with a limited grasp of the English language, which can make things more difficult but not impossible. Cast Members do speak many other languages too – Spanish and Italian are common.

USEFUL FRENCH PHRASES:

Hello/Good morning – *Bonjour [Bon-sjur]*
Good evening – *Bonsoir [Bon-swar]*
Do you speak English? – Parlez-vous anglais? *[Par-lay voo-zarn-glay]*
How much does this cost? – Ça coûte combien? *[Sar Coot Com-byer]*
Please – S'il vous plait *[Sill voo-play]*
Thanks – Merci! *[Mair-si]*
No problem – De rien *[De ree-yeah]*
A photo of us please? – Une photo s'il vous plaît? *[Oon photo sill voo-play]*
Yes – Oui *[We]*
No – Non *[No – do not pronounce the final 'n']*
A little / a bit – Un peu *[Um purr]*
Rare (for meat) – *Saignante [Say-narnte]*
Medium-Rare (for meat) – À pointe *[Ah pwarnt]*
Well-done/well-cooked (for meat) – *Bien Cuite [Bee-yen kweet]*
Very well-cooked (for meat) – *Très Bien Cuite [Treh bee-yen kweet]*

Time Zones

France uses the UTC+1 time zone, which is used throughout most of Central and Western Europe. The UK and Portugal operate on UTC time and therefore 1:00pm in the UK is 2:00pm in France.

Some countries in Eastern Europe such as Ukraine and Latvia use the UTC+2 time zone so 3:00pm in Latvia is 2:00pm in France.

We recommend that you set your watches, alarm clocks and mobile phone clocks to French time as soon as you board your flight, train or ferry to France – or as soon as you cross the French border for those travelling by car.

By doing this you will make sure that you are in the correct time zone for things such as check-in times, opening hours and Fastpass return times.

This is also vital to make sure you do not miss your return flights, ferries or trains on the way back home.

Currency and Payment Methods

France uses Euros as its currency. If you come from a country that does not use Euros as its currency, then you can either exchange cash before you go, or use a debit card or credit card to pay for your purchases whilst in France.

However, be aware that most banks add additional fees when paying by card in a foreign currency.

Be sure to warn your bank you will be visiting France to avoid your card being blocked as banks may fear your card has been stolen.

Traveller's cheques are accepted at Disneyland Paris but we do not recommend these. We recommend using a Pre-paid debit card from a company such as FairFX (UK readers only, but other similar companies are available in other countries).

These pre-paid cards allow you to top-up the card with as many Euros as you would like, like a mobile phone top up works. You can then use the card for purchases with no additional fees when abroad and recharge the card at any time.

If you do plan on using FairFx, there is usually a £9.95 card purchase fee. However, if you use our special link at http://bit.ly/debitdlp - the card

purchase fee magically disappears. Plus, our link also includes bonus cash for top-ups over £250.

For guests who prefer to exchange money at the theme parks, there are Bureau de Changes located at both theme parks and in the Disney Village. These operate limited opening hours – in addition, the rates offered are not usually quite poor.

Wheelchair and Pushchair Rentals

Wheelchair and pushchair rentals are available at Disneyland Paris for those who do not wish to bring their own with them.

If your child is recently out of a pushchair, it may still be worth renting one as it is likely they will get tired, due to the huge walking distances involved with a Disneyland Paris visit.

Sometimes it is nice to just let them sit in their pushchair and have a break. They can also be used as a way to carry around bags.

It should be noted that Disneyland Paris' pushchairs do not recline, and do not have any real rain protection. Many guests also say that the pushchairs are not the most comfortable.

The daily cost for hiring a wheelchair or pushchair is €15. The deposit required for a wheelchair is €150; this is €70 for a pushchair if you wish to be able to take it out of the parks, move between parks or enter the Disney Village.

You are, of course, welcome to bring your own pushchair or wheelchair with you if you wish.

When experiencing attractions, be sure to leave your pushchair in the dedicated parking areas. Ask a Cast Member if you are not sure whether this is. Pushchairs may be moved by Cast Members to keep them neat and organised.

Celebrating Birthdays

There are several ways to celebrate a birthday at Disneyland Paris. For example, if you are dining at any Table Service restaurant, you can add a birthday cake to your meal for €29.

We recommend making a restaurant reservation by calling the dining booking line and mentioning the cake in advance.

Additionally, guests can visit City Hall and Studio Services to be given a 'Happy Birthday' badge to wear throughout the day.

To keep the younger guests happy, make sure to ask the Cast Members at City Hall whether any of the characters have a special birthday message for your child. You will be lead into a room, and then the phone will ring. When your child picks the phone up there will be a recorded message wishing them a happy birthday – this can make for some incredible memories.

Lockers

When Disneyland Paris originally opened in 1992, there were lockers located inside Disneyland Park.

However, security has tightened up over recent years and there are now no self-storage luggage services inside the theme parks themselves. Instead, there are two luggage services located just outside the theme park entrances where you hand your bag to a Cast Member and they put it in storage behind the counter.

At Disneyland Park 'Luggage Services' is located to the right of the main entrance by the Guest Relations window. This is by the entrance to the Disneyland Hotel.

At Walt Disney Studios Park, luggage storage is to the right of the ticket windows.

There is also an automatic left luggage storage facility available inside *Marne-La-Vallee – Chessy* rail station on the upper level. Disneyland Paris does not operate the service in the train station.

Lockers at the parks and in the station range in price from €5 to €10 depending on the size of locker and number of bags stored.

For the station lockers, you need exact change (there is a change machine inside the locker room), whereas at the Disney Parks you can pay in cash or by card.

Dream Annual Passport holders may store one item in left luggage per day at the parks at no cost.

You can access the Disneyland Paris park lockers as many times as you want throughout the day to get items without being charged more than once. With the station lockers, every time you open the lockers, you must pay again to lock them. Plus, you must go back and forth through Disneyland Paris security checkpoint each time.

Important: Selfie sticks and camera extension poles are banned in the theme parks. If you have once, you can keep it in the locker storage at both parks for free.

Frequently Asked Questions

Can I leave and re-enter the park on the same day?
Yes, of course you can.

Can I take my own food into the theme parks?
Yes. The bag searches in operation are for safety reasons and not to prevent you from taking food or drinks into the parks.

You can take snacks, sandwiches and drinks into the parks, as well as baby milk, which restaurants will happily heat for you.

Picnics are forbidden so do not expect to lay down a blanket and have a meal on the grass in the theme parks. Find a bench instead – we particularly like the area near the Frontierland Disneyland Railroad station due to the large amount of seating available.

Additionally, there is a picnic area located outside the theme parks – simply ask a Cast Member at the exit of the parks.

Glass containers and bottles are not allowed in the parks.

Are there any baby facilities?
Each park has its own Baby Care Centre with microwaves, bottle warmers, high chairs, and changing tables. These locations are designed to be comfortable and quiet, and can be a good escape from the noise of the parks.

Nappies and baby food are also on sale at some locations.

What if I fall ill or get injured?
Disneyland Paris makes safety its number one priority and everything is done to ensure you have a safe visit. Unfortunately, it is possible that some guests may fall ill or become injured while at the resort – each park has a First Aid Centre with qualified medical staff to help you with any problems.

If more serious intervention is required, Disneyland Paris has its own licensed emergency services department, and also works very closely with outside hospitals and agencies.

Is there a prayer room?
There is not a dedicated prayer room within the theme parks. Please visit City Hall or Studio Services where they can arrange for a room for you to use.

Are there any local religious restrictions?
According to the gov.uk travel advice website: "Concealing the face in public places in France is illegal. This includes balaclavas, full veils or any other garment or mask that is used to conceal the face. Failure to comply with the ban is punishable by a maximum fine of €150."

"Under this law, forcing someone to hide their face is also a crime and is punishable by a year's imprisonment and a fine of up to €30,000. If the person forced to hide their face is a minor, the sentence is doubled. The law does not provide any exemption for tourists."

This is not a choice Disney has made, but the government's – at Disneyland Paris, however, you *will* find some guests covering their face for religious reasons; they will not be fined when on private property such as Disneyland Paris.

How to Queue Less

Disneyland Paris meticulously themes its queues to begin to tell the story of the attraction you about to experience before you board. However, often you just want to get on the ride as quickly as possible.

It is important to remember that a visit to a theme park will inevitably involve waiting in queue lines. This chapter covers our top tips on minimising these waits.

1 Eat outside the normal dining hours

At Disneyland Paris, it is normal to queue to order your food. Whether you want to eat at a Table Service restaurant or a Quick Service meal, waiting is part of the game. Have lunch before midday or after 3:00pm for much shorter waits. In addition, having dinner before 7:00pm will also guarantee that you wait less. A wait of 45 minutes or longer at Quick Service restaurants is fairly typical at peak times.

2 Quick Service meal tricks

At Quick Service locations, cashiers have two queues and alternate between them – count how many groups (families) are in front of you in the queue. There may be ten people in front of you in one queue line but only two families. The other queue line may have five people, but from five different families. The queue with ten people moves quicker with only two orders to process, whereas the other queue has five.

3 On-site Disney hotel guests

If you are staying at an on-site Disneyland Paris hotel, take advantage of the great Extra Magic Hours. You get entry into one of the theme parks up to two hours before regular guests do. During this time, you can experience many of the park's attractions with minimal waits. See our Extra Magic Hours section for more details.

4 Disneyland Park opens early

Disneyland Park's opening hours usually state it officially opens at 10:00am, but any guest can enter the park 30 minutes earlier. This means you can enter the park, enjoy the atmosphere, eat breakfast, start shopping and take photos of Main Street, U.S.A. and Sleeping Beauty Castle. In front of the castle, the entrances to all the lands will be cordoned off by Cast Members.

If you are a Disney hotel guest or a Fantasy or Dream annual pass holder, show your Magic Card or annual pass and you can enter Fantasyland and Discoveryland. Otherwise, wait by the ropes at the entrances of the lands for "rope-drop" as the park opens. If you are there before the park opens, you can be on your first ride in minutes.

5 Walt Disney Studios Park opens early

Walt Disney Studios Park also opens at 9:30am. At that time, you can walk around the entire park and queue outside attraction entrances. Most attractions will not start operating until the park's official opening, but some regularly open early. You should use this time to get in the queue outside the entrance to *Crush's Coaster*.

6 Crush's Coaster does not have Fastpass

If you plan on experiencing *Crush's Coaster*, we cannot overstate how important it is for you to be at Walt Disney Studios Park's turnstiles before 9:30am. By doing this you will be able to go through the turnstiles when the park pre-opens and make your way to *Crush's Coaster*. This attraction usually starts operating slightly before the park officially opens. See 'Chapter 10: Touring Plans' for more details on how to maximise your time at the park. Alternatively, use the Single Rider queue line to save a lot of time.

7 Skip the parades and fireworks

If you have already seen the parades, shows or fireworks, use that time to ride attractions as the wait times are often much shorter during these big events. If you have not seen the park's entertainment offerings before, we do not recommend you skip them. Parades and shows are only performed at set times of the day and most of these are as good as, if not better, than many rides.

8 Ride outdoor attractions when it rains

Outdoor attractions such as *Dumbo, Flying Carpets over Agrabah, Casey Junior, Storybook Canal boats, Big Thunder Mountain, Indiana Jones et le Temple du Peril, Lancelot's Carousel* (outdoor queue), *Slinky Dog Zigzag Spin, Toy Soldiers Parachute Drop* and *RC Racer* have significantly reduced waits when it is raining. Yes, you may get soaked whilst riding (a poncho can help with this) but the wait times will be lower.

Top Tip: Many guests return to the hotels if it begins raining, so many of the indoor rides will also have shorter queues when there is inclement weather.

9 Choose when to visit carefully

Visit during an off-peak time if possible. If you are visiting on New Year's Day, expect to queue a lot longer than in the middle of February, and of course weekends are busier than weekdays. See our 'When to Visit' section to make the most of your time.

10 Shop at the start or end of the day

If you enter the park during the pre-opening period from 9:30am to 10:00am, this is a perfect time to go shopping. Alternatively, go shopping at the end of the day. Even when the park is 'officially' closed, the shops on Main Street, U.S.A. stay open up to an hour longer than the rest of the park. Alternatively, just walk over to Disney Village in the evening, and go shopping there until midnight or 1:00am on most days!

Additionally, the on-site hotels and some partner hotels have a small Disney boutique inside them. Do not waste your time during the day shopping, do it at strategic times and make the most of your time in the parks.

11 Get a Times Guide

Get your Park Map and the Times Guide on the way in; you will usually find them being distributed together. The Times Guide lists all time-sensitive information at the parks such as the timings of parades, shows, character appearances and more. As such, you will not waste time crossing the park to find out that a character you saw earlier in the day has now left a particular location.

Disneyland Paris for Walt Disney World Regulars

Many guests visit Disneyland Paris after having visited the Walt Disney World Resort in Florida. Both resorts immerse yourself in the Disney magic, but it is important to understand that the two locations are very different. This chapter helps you compare the resorts.

The Cast Members and Languages

The Cast Members in Florida and California, for the most part, go above and beyond, are extremely polite, are never rude to a guest, have a passion for Disney and do everything to make your stay as magical as possible.

However, the Cast Members in the US are very restricted by the Disney rulebook, which even affects their personal lives such as how they can cut and style their hair.

Disneyland Paris is a Disney Park for the 21st century where a 'Disney Look' dictating employees personal appearance is illegal. French employment laws are very strict, so Cast Members cannot be reprimanded for not smiling or for leaning at work.

In addition, French customer service is almost non-existent compared to American standards. Having said this, most of the Paris Cast are pleasant, inviting and helpful – just do not expect American standards in France.

Cast Members in Paris generally speak several languages, and having a chat with one of the Cast could lead to you booking your next vacation to somewhere you would never have thought of visiting.

All Cast Members must speak at least two major European languages, including French.

Almost the entire Cast speak English well, but it is not mandatory. You may, on a rare occasion, encounter a Cast Member that does not speak English, so it pays to learn some basic French.

It is basic manners to learn some of the language when visiting another country and at least say *Bonjour* and *Merci*.

Local Customs

According to the last available figures from Disneyland Paris, 48% of all visitors to the resort are French, and 16% are from the UK. Other countries with a high number of guests include Spain and Italy.

Disneyland Paris has a very high proportion of European visitors, unlike Walt Disney World's visitors from all corners of the world (but mainly Americans).

Many American customs do not apply to a European audience. One of these is waiting in a queue. Many Europeans do not queue in daily life. Instead, people gather in small groups instead of an orderly queue. For example, when a bus arrives, it is a free-for-all and people rush for the doors with no regard for those waiting the longest.

For characters that make random appearances in the parks, you can expect a crowd of parents pushing their children to get their photo taken first. When a queue is set up, though, Europeans seem to be fine at complying.

Tipping is also different. Meals in France have a tip included in the price so there is no need to tip. This compares to the US, where tips of 15% or 20% of a meal's price are expected.

In general, guests are much less respectful at the Parisian parks – they climb into cordoned off areas, sit anywhere they can, and they smoke freely in the parks despite it being banned.

Guests in Europe expect to have an alcoholic beverage with their meal – as such, you will find beer on sale at Quick Service locations. Wine and other alcoholic beverages are also offered at all Table Service locations.

In general Europeans are more used to drinking alcohol with a meal than Americans; the sale of alcoholic drinks has not had a negative effect on the parks.

Lastly, the European audience are a little bit more fashion conscious than the crowds that visit Florida. Ponchos, for example, are sold at Disneyland Paris, but they are more than often replaced by umbrellas and raincoats in Europe.

Having said this there is more than a fair share of guests dressed "interestingly" at Disneyland Paris.

Weather

Florida is known as the "sunshine state" and you can expect temperatures to reach 30°C (80-90°F) for much of the year.

There are occasions where there are cold snaps and the temperature drops for a few days, but nothing to the levels seen in Paris.

Paris' weather is much more variable; the average daily temperature in Paris in July and August is about 25°C (77°F) whereas temperatures in January and February average at 3°CC (37°F), often dipping below freezing.

Visitors to Walt Disney World have to deal with Hurricane season much of the year (June to November) when weather can get extreme, and hurricanes are possible. These are unheard of in Paris.

Orlando visitors also deal with a tropical climate with daily thunderstorms in the summer, closing all outdoor attractions and drenching anyone not prepared. Paris' rain is more unpredictable, and is present year-round.

Resort Size and Transportation

This is the main difference between Walt Disney World and Disneyland Paris. Walt Disney World is 47 square miles or 121 square kilometres.

In comparison, Disneyland Paris is 22.3 square kilometres. The difference is staggering.

From the furthest resort hotels to the parks is no more than a 20-minute walk at Disneyland Paris or a five-minute bus journey.

However, at Walt Disney World it could be a 20-minute bus journey to a park; most distances cannot be walked - not only because of the distance but because their are no pavements connecting most areas due to the sprawling size of Walt Disney World.

At Disneyland Paris, the two theme parks are within walking distance, as is the Disney Village. Everything is a bus journey way from each other at Walt Disney World.

The advantage of Disneyland Paris' small size is that you can walk throughout the whole resort, you can visit any of the other hotels easily, and you will spend less time traveling and more time enjoying yourself.

The disadvantage at Disneyland Paris is that the choice of things to do is much more limited: there are no water parks, there are fewer hotels to choose from, and crucially there are fewer theme parks (there are only two in Paris, as opposed to four in Florida). Overall, there are fewer things to do at Disneyland Paris due to its smaller size.

Looking at the parks, Disneyland Park is slightly bigger than Magic Kingdom Park, but with emptier, quieter areas and fewer rides. The walkways in the park feel significantly less crowded in Paris.

Walt Disney Studios Park in Paris is about half the size of Disney's Hollywood Studios in Orlando. The resort hotels in Paris are also generally smaller than their Floridian counterparts.

If you have visited the Disneyland Resort in California, Disneyland Paris is much more comparable to it – everything is within walking distance. Paris' resort is larger than the Disneyland Resort, however.

The area where Disneyland Paris is located is as much a major transport hub, as it is a world-class theme park resort.

On Disneyland Paris property, just two minutes from the park entrances, you can hop on a high speed TGV train to travel across France, or a Eurostar train to the UK.

Alternatively, you can use the regional RER trains and travel into central Paris in just 35 minutes, to experience one of the most beautiful cities in the world.

You can also drive from your hotel and be at a non-Disney location in just a couple of minutes too.

Disneyland Paris is all very self-contained so if you do fancy escaping the magic, it is easy to do so unlike in Florida! For some people this freedom is a benefit, though others prefer the Floridian immersion of the Disney magic that really lets them forget about the outside world.

Pricing

A visit to Disneyland Paris can be very pricey when you take into account all of the costs.

Room prices at on-site hotels include tickets to the theme parks for the length of stay. However, you will not find a room at a Disney hotel for under £200 or $220 per night – and these are the absolute cheapest rooms during off-peak seasons.

In contrast, the cheapest hotels in Walt Disney World are half of this price, though park tickets are not included. At Disneyland Paris, there are almost always special offers available, so be sure to not book at full rate.

A one-day entry ticket to Disneyland Paris for one park is €75 (£59 or $79) for adults and €63 for children. A two-park hopper is €90 (£71 or $94) and €66 respectively. The daily rate drastically reduces the longer you visit the resort. A 5-day ticket is €229 (£180 or $242) for adults.

For comparison, at Walt Disney World, a one day, one park adult ticket is $103 to $132 dollars with tax, or a park hopper (for four theme parks) is $165 to $175. A 5-day ticket is $362 for one park per day, or $435 with the park hopper option).

In general, Walt Disney World tickets are more expensive, though there is much more to do at the theme parks there.

Longer stays of 7 or 14-days in Florida become more affordable per day.

Food prices at Disneyland Paris, however, are expensive in comparison to the US and many people bring picnic food into the parks for this reason.

A burger, fries and drink combo will set you back about €14 (£11/$15) at Disneyland Paris. A burger and fries in the US will cost you about $10 without a drink or about $13 with one.

At Table Service establishments, the price difference is even more notable. A Set Menu at a good in-park restaurant will set you back €50 to €60 ($52 to $63) at Disneyland Paris. The equivalent at Walt Disney World would be about 30% cheaper.

This adds up to a big price difference when ordering for a family of four over several days.

Don't expect signature foods like Dole Whips and Mickey Premium Bars in Disneyland Paris, either.

Fastpass

Fastpass at Disneyland Paris works in the same way the paper Fastpass system used to work in Walt Disney World. You go to a Fastpass machine, insert your ticket and get a return time.

Florida's paper Fastpass system was replaced by a digital Fastpass+ system in 2014. With Fastpass+ you can make ride reservations on your smartphone or using in-park kiosks up to 60 days in advance, or on

the day itself.

Another difference is that at Disneyland Paris, the return time windows are only 30 minutes long instead of the 1-hour in the US parks.

Unique Attractions and Details

Disneyland Paris has some unique rides and shows that just cannot be found at Walt Disney World.

In Disneyland Park *Phantom Manor*, is a beautiful rendition of the classic Haunted Mansion ride with a new storyline and an entirely different interior but keeping some familiar elements.

Pirates of the Caribbean is much longer, has a better queue, new scenes and bigger drops in Paris.

Star Wars Hyperspace Mountain is beautiful in Paris from the outside and it is an incredibly intense looping roller Coaster inside, that blows its Floridian counterpart out of the water; and *Big Thunder Mountain* is great fun in Paris and is set in the middle of an island.

Furthermore, there are lots of unique walkthroughs such as *The Nautilus* and *Alice's Curious Labyrinth* too. *Casey Junior* and *Storybook Canal Boats* also do not exist in Florida.

Indiana Jones et le Temple du Peril is also a unique roller Coaster. There is, however, no 'New Fantasyland expansion' in Paris. The *Disney Illuminations* night-time spectacular is like a mix of all of Walt Disney World's night-time shows rolled into one.

In Walt Disney Studios Park, *Crush's Coaster* is a unique spinning roller Coaster in the dark and *Cars Quatre Roues Rallye* is a unique tea-cup style ride themed to *Cars*.

The *Art of Disney Animation* exists in Paris after it was shuttered in Florida – the same applies to *Studio Tram Tour*.

Toy Story Playland has three unique rides, and *Animagique* Theatre is home to a unique stage show. *Stitch Live* is a cool interactive show, similar to Turtle Talk with Crush.

Finally, *Ratatouille: The Adventure* is a world-class, dark ride unlike anything in the US parks.

Disneyland Park is absolutely beautiful. Everything is incredibly elaborately themed, sharing inspiration from the US parks whilst introducing exotic elements that cannot be found elsewhere.

In comparison, Walt Disney Studios Park is filled with concrete and metallic structures everywhere, with very few thematic details. Although, over the past five years there has been an effort to improve the park, it is clear that Walt Disney Studios Park lacks the detail that makes Disney theme parks unique.

Even Hollywood Studios, which is in our opinion the worst-themed park at Walt Disney World, has superior theming to the Studios park in Paris. The number of attractions at both the Studios parks is paltry.

The hotels at Disneyland Paris are American-themed, but do not live up to the resort hotels found at Walt Disney World. The hotels in Paris are just hotels, whereas you could spend several days at the hotel resorts in the US and enjoy the surroundings and experiences on offer.

The Seasons and The Future

Disneyland Paris offers its guests something different throughout the year, with seasonal and special events that celebrate traditions such as St. Patrick's Day, Halloween and Christmas. This section explores all of these. Then, we take a look at the future of the resort.

Season of the Force

14th January to 26th March 2017 and January to March 2018

For the first time ever, in 2017, Disneyland Paris awakens with the Season of the Force. The season will include:

"Star Wars: A Galactic Celebration" Nighttime Show - Make your way to Walt Disney Studios Park for a sensational show in front of Hollywood Tower Hotel, as light projection, special effects and live characters turn darkness into spectacular scenes from the Star Wars saga. This "360-degree" show will provide "perfect immersion" in the Star Wars Universe.

Expect to see Chewbacca, R2-D2, Kylo Ren, Darth Maul, Darth Vader and more in person during this show.

"Star Wars: A Galaxy Far, Far Away" Stage Show - Let the Force guide you to Production Courtyard in Walt Disney Studios Park for an extraordinary example of galactic might. Will you submit to the dark side? Or does your path lead to the light side?

This show puts the spotlight on a number of iconic characters from the saga, such as Darth Vader and Kylo Ren, to name but a few.

Stormtrooper March - Blast off to Walt Disney Studios Park and witness the wicked wonder of Captain Phasma leading a battalion of stormtroopers on an iconic military march - and they're on the hunt for rebel spies.

All elements of "Season of the Force" will actually stay around after this season ends and until 30th September 2017, with the exception of the nighttime show which will only be performed during this season.

St. David's Welsh Festival

3rd to 5th March 2017

This three day long mini-season has been traditionally celebrated in Frontierland, at Disneyland Park.

During the Festival, guests can take photos with some of their favourite

Disney characters clad in traditional Welsh robes.

In addition, Disneyland Paris usually has traditional Welsh singers, such as a choir, perform at the festival several times throughout the day.

Traditional music, a crafts market, traditional food and drink, complimentary face painting, and a special St. David's fireworks display make the festival a great unique event.

St. Patrick's Day

17th March 2017

Much like the St. David's Day celebrations featured above, this one-day celebration of all things Celtic takes place in Frontierland, at Disneyland

Park.

Guests can enjoy live traditional music, photo opportunities, character appearances, a pre-

parade, and a special St. Patrick's Day fireworks display.

Disneyland Paris Marathon
21st to 24th September 2017

In 2016, Disneyland Paris launched its first even major fitness event with a focus on running. The event returns in 2017.

• **Kick Off Party** (22nd September 2017) – On Friday evening, Disney Characters, exclusive access to attractions, and plenty of food and drinks will be part of the private party held in Walt Disney Studios Park from 21:00 to 0:00. This is priced at €49.

• **5km Run** (22nd September 2017) – A 5km (3.1mi) run starting at 8:00pm. The 5km race will go through Walt Disney Studios Park with characters along the route. Open from ages 5 and up.

• **Kids Races** (23rd September 2017) – Kids races will take place from 11:00am and are only for children under 12. There will be 100m, 200m and 1km races.

• **10km Run** (23rd September 2017) – New for 2017, this 10km (6.2 mi) run will take place exclusively inside the grounds of Disneyland Paris with characters along the route.

• **Half Marathon** (24th September 2017) – The main 13.1-mile half-marathon race (21.1km) will be held on Sunday 24th, starting at 7:00am. It will take you through both Disney theme parks, Disney hotels, as well as the local villages surrounding the theme parks.

Disney characters will be stationed throughout the race route. The Half Marathon race is open to ages 18+ only and a medical certificate is required.

• **RunDisney Health & Fitness Expo** – This will run from 21st to 24th September 2017 in the Disney Events Arena. Here participants can get their race T-shirt, race number bib and gear bags. Plus, everyone can get a peek at the latest in fitness apparel, footwear, sunglasses, high tech gadgets, and nutritional products.

The Expo will also showcase a Speaker Series that includes appearances by celebrity runners and seminars on training, running, and nutrition featuring speakers and panellists from the running industry.

Race participants will also get a medal for each race they complete and refreshments during and after their race. A special '10km + Half Marathon' medal will be available for those who complete both races.

Travel package bookings for the 2017 race opened up on 22nd November 2016, and individual race-only registrations will launch in February or March 2017. In 2016, all the race-only places sold out on release day.

Packages include hotel stays, park tickets and the race entry price.

Race-only prices for 2017 are: €75 for the half-marathon, €55 for the 10km run, €35 for the 5km run and €12 for the kids run.

A race-only Photopass is available for €39, and a 'race plus park' Photopass is €69.

Halloween
1st October to 5th November 2017

Disneyland Paris' Halloween season is one of the most elaborate celebrations at the resort, with unique shows, parades, décors and more to delight guests.

This information is for the 2016 Halloween season. Some events may not return for the 2017 season, and new events may be added but this sets expectations as Halloween is very similar each year.

"It's Good to Be Bad with the Disney Villains" Show and Happening – On Castle Stage in front of the castle in the afternoons, the villains sing and dance in a short stage show. They then descend for meet and greets. The show is repeated with a different villain hosting each time.

"Mickey's Box of Pumpkins" – Meet Mickey in his Halloween attire at *Cottonwood Creek Ranch* in Frontierland.

Maleficent's Court – Maleficent meets guests from mid-morning until before the parade in the courtyard area at the back of Sleeping Beauty Castle.

Mickey's Halloween Cavalcade Celebration – This mini-parade themed to the autumn harvest passes through the park several times per day. See Mickey, Minnie, the three little pigs, Horace Horsecollar, Clarabelle Cow and other characters and dancers. *Disney Stars on Parade* is also performed once daily at Halloween.

Decorations, Food and Merchandise – Main Street, U.S.A. is invaded by ghostly decorations for some great photo opportunities. Frontierland is also well-decorated. Disney characters also sport Halloween-themed costumes. Villains-themed merchandise and special Halloween inspired menus are available.

Stitch and Minnie's Costume Couture – Meet Minnie by Casey's Corner on Main Street, USA. Stitch is also present at this photo location to meet guests.

Jack and Sally's Cemetery (from *The Nightmare Before Christmas*) – Meet Jack and Sally at their Halloween themed location in Frontierland.

Goofy's Candy Factory – Goofy wears his Halloween gear in Town Square, ready for photos with you by his candy machine.

Disney's Halloween Party: On 31st October between 8:30pm and 1:00am, this ticketed event offers an evening of frightening entertainment. Details are from the 2016 event and may change in 2017.

Most Disneyland Park attractions are open during the event and guests may wear Halloween costumes (subject to restrictions).

Entry is £34/€45 for the evening for guests aged 3 and up. Under 3s go free. Guests may enter from 5:00pm with party tickets.

Special entertainment is available during the party including character meet and greets, Minnie's Pirate Academy show, a Disco party, and Mickey's Halloween Celebration cavalcade.

Mickey's Magical Fireworks and Bonfire

6th, 8th & 10th November 2017

See the night sky t transformed above Lake Disney as Disney sets its fireworks off to music to celebrate Bonfire Night. The show lasts approximately 20 minutes.

Lake Disney is by the on-site Disney hotels - no park entry is required and admission is free.

Christmas

11th November 2017 to 7th January 2018

For the most magical time of the year, make Disneyland Paris your stop. Here you are guaranteed snow every day, magical characters and unforgettable experiences.

The following details are for the 2016 Christmas season. Traditionally, the Christmas seasons do not change hugely from year to year so you can expect much of this information to be valid for the 2017

Christmas season too. Information on the 2017 season will not be unveiled before September 2017 at the earliest.

The park will be filled with Christmas touches everywhere you go but no more so than Main Street, U.S.A - here you will find a giant Christmas tree, snowmen on each corner and baubles and tinsel abound.

Royal Christmas Wishes – The Castle stage comes to life with all your favourite Princes and Princesses in this show, including Aurora, Belle, Snow White, Ariel, Cinderella, Rapunzel, Tiana, Jasmine, and their accompanying Princes.

Disney's Christmas Parade – This Christmas-themed parade marches down Fantasyland and Main Street, U.S.A. The parade stars Father Christmas until Christmas day. The regular parade, *Disney Stars on Parade* is also performed once daily during the Christmas season.

Frozen Sing-Along – This popular sing-along show is back for the Christmas season. It is performed six times a day in the week, and twelve times a day on weekends and peak days. In addition, *Frozen: A Royal Welcome* sees the sisters parade through the park twice a day.

Mickey's Magical Christmas Lights – Every evening as the night falls, the park's signature Christmas tree comes to life with the help of Mickey, Minnie and Santa in this new illumination ceremony. The show takes place daily.

Meet Santa – You can meet both Santa and Mickey at *Meet Mickey Mouse*. There are two queue lines – one for Mickey photos and the other for Santa photos.

Disney Dreams of Christmas – This Christmas version of the night-time spectacular combines projections, water jets, special effects and pyrotechnics. Together they will bring Sleeping Beauty Castle to life with the help of Olaf from *Frozen*, as guests celebrate Christmas traditions from around the world and see winter-themed scenes from Disney classics.

The show is still not as good as the regular Disney Illuminations show performed during the rest of the year, in our opinion. It is, however, a stunning way to cap off a Christmas-season day at the parks.

Meet Jack Skellington – Meet Jack from *The Nightmare Before Christmas* in his 'Sandy Claws' outfit in Frontierland.

Special Dinners – In Europe, Christmas Eve and New Year's Eve dinners are a big family affair. As such, dinners on these days are available at a heavy

supplement.

Prices vary from £89 (€129) to £211 (€259) per adult on Christmas Eve. On Christmas day a special 4-course lunch is available for £139 per adult. New Year's Eve meals range in price from £97 (€119) to £243 (€299) per adult.

Full details on these meals are available over the phone or in the latest Disneyland Paris brochure.

Personally we think these prices are ludicrous with a family of 4 spending at least €400 on a single meal. Our recommendation is to eat in one of the Quick Service restaurants to avoid these hefty price tags (or at a Table Service location as a late lunch).

Alternatively, choose from one of the Table Service restaurants not doing special dinners, or eat in the Disney Village at selected restaurants. Reservations are strongly recommended.

New Year's Eve
31st December

Celebrate the start of the New Year at Disneyland Paris.

This is traditionally the busiest day at the resort and you can expect the theme parks to reach maximum capacity with very long wait times for all

rides.

If you can put up with that, you can experience a fireworks display at either Disneyland Park, Walt Disney Studios Park or at Lake Disney (no admission cost at this last location).

The theme parks are open until 1:00am meaning you have one hour of post-fireworks attraction time..

All the Christmas entertainment is still running on this date, and continues into early January.

The Future - Projects in Progress & Rumours

Walt Disney Studios Park Expansion – Walt Disney studios Park is set to continue to expand in size, and with additional attractions.

It is even possible that the entire theme park will get a re-theme, though nothing has been confirmed.

Some of the projects that are rumoured to arrive include *Toy Story Midway Mania*, and a re-theme of the entire Backlot area to Marvel.

It is possible that construction for a new attraction may begin in 2017, opening for Spring 2019.

Ten Big Refurbishments – Disneyland Paris has been renovating for the 25th anniversary. Work will continue until mid-2017. The following attractions are still set to be enhanced as of the time of publication.

• *Space Mountain* – Phase 2 closure from January to May 2017. New, more comfortable trains are expected. The ride will re-open as *Hyperspace Mountain*, themed to Star Wars.
• *Studio Tram Tour: Behind the Magic* – Closed from January to April 2017.
• *Pirates of the Caribbean* – Closed from January 2017 to Summer 2017. New effects and the addition of Jack Sparrow animatronics are expected.

Disney Village expansion – Disney Village is set to be expanded over the coming years, with new shopping and dining experiences. Vapiano, an Italian food chain, has already opened, as has Five Guys Burgers & Fries. A third dining location is also expected to open in 2017.

Technological updates – Free public Wi-Fi is due to be introduced at the parks in early 2017.

Hotels – Disneyland Paris has been refurbishing all of its hotels over the past few years. Currently, the Hotel Cheyenne's rooms are being refurbished until September 2017. During renovations, all the hotel amenities will be available at usual.

In 2018 Hotel New York will close for a complete overhaul, followed by the Disneyland Hotel.

In addition, there are plans for a new "value"-priced on-site hotel. Construction has not started so this could still be many years off.

A Special Thanks

Thank you very much for reading our travel guide. We hope this book has made a big difference to your trip to Disneyland Paris, and that you have found some tips that will save you time, money and hassle! Remember to take this guide with you when you are visiting the resort. This guide is also available in a digital format.

If you have any feedback about any element of the guide, or have noticed changes in the parks that differ from what is in the book, do let us know by sending us a message. To contact us, visit our website at www.independentguidebooks.com/contact-us/

If you enjoyed the guide, we would love for you to leave a review on Amazon or wherever you have purchased this guide from. Your reviews make a huge difference in helping other people find this guide. Thank you.

Have a magical time!

If you have enjoyed this guide, other travel guides in this series include:

- The Independent Guide to Walt Disney World
- The Independent Guide to Universal Orlando
- The Independent Guide to Universal Studios Hollywood
- The Independent Guide to Disneyland
- The Independent Guide to Hong Kong
- The Independent Guide to Tokyo
- The Independent Guide to Dubai
- The Independent Guide to Paris
- The Independent Guide to London
- The Independent Guide to New York City

Photo credits:

The following photos have been used from Flickr (unless otherwise stated) in this guide under a Creative Commons license. Thank you to: Sleeping Beauty Castle (cover) - Heather Cowpter, Tower of Terror (cover) - David Jafra, Eurostar (small) - 'kismihok; Eurostar (large) - Philip Sheldrake; Thunder Mesa Riverboat, Buffalo Bills, Blanche Neige and La Cabane des Robinson - Loren Javier; Dumbo & Pinocchio - Jeremy Thompson; Nautilus - Paul Beattie; Star Tours - Anna Fox; and Ratatouille exterior - Eleazar; Fastpass (single) - Joel; Fastpass (multiple) - JJ Merelo; View of Lake Disney (La Marina section) - Nicola; Val d'EOPE - Tves Jalabert; Davy Crockett's Adventure - aventure-aventure.com; Golf - DisneylandParis.com; Aerial Image - Apple Maps; Disney Dollars - R Reeves; Teacups - Kabayanmark Images. Some images are copyright The Walt Disney Company, Disneyland Paris and EuroDisney SCA.

Disneyland Park Map

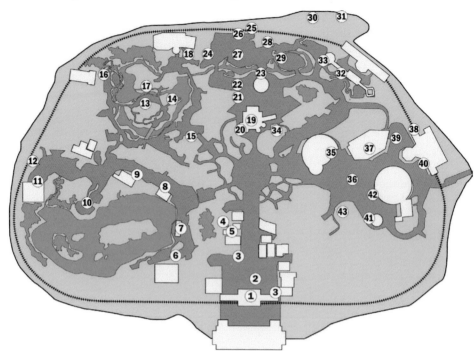

1 - Main Street, U.S.A. Station
2 - Horse-Drawn Streetcars
3 - Main Street Vehicles
4 - Liberty Arcade (Statue of Liberty Tableau)
5 - Dapper Dan's Hair Cuts
6 - Phantom Manor
7 - Thunder Mesa Riverboat Landing
8 - Rustler Roundup Shooting Gallery
9 - Big Thunder Mountain
10 - Pocahontas Indian Village
11 - Chaparral Theatre
12 - Frontierland Station
13 - La Cabane des Robinson (Treehouse)

14 - Pirates' Beach
15 - Le Passage Enchante d'Aladdin
16 - Indiana Jones et le Temple du Peril
17 - Adventure Isle
18 - Pirates of the Caribbean
19 - Sleeping Beauty Castle
20 - Dragon's Lair
21 - Snow White and the Seven Dwarfs
22 - Pinocchio's Fantastic Journey
23 - Lancelot's Carousel
24 - Peter Pan's Flight
25 - Fantasyland Station
26 - Meet Mickey
27 - Dumbo: The Flying Elephant
28 - Alice's Curious Labyrinth

29 - Mad Hatter's Tea Cups
30 - Casey Jr.
31 - Storybook Canal Boats
32 - "it's a small world"
33 - Princess Pavilion
34 - Castle Stage
35 - Buzz Lightyear Laser Blast
36 - Orbitron
37 - Videopolis
38 - Discoveryland Station
39 - Star Tours
40 - Discoveryland Theatre
41 - Nautilus
42 - Star Wars Hyperspace Mountain
43 - Autopia

Walt Disney Studios Park Map

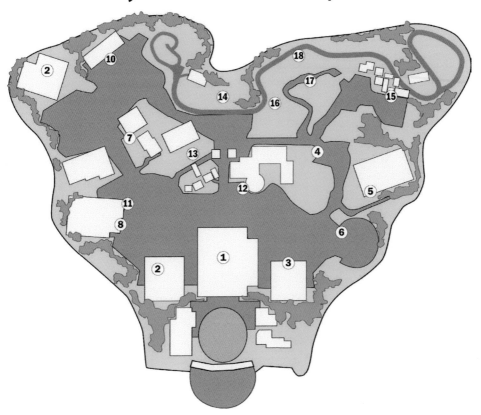

1 - Disney Studio 1
2 - CineMagique Theatre
3 - Animagique Theatre
4 - Cars Race Rallye
5 - Crush's Coaster
6 - Flying Carpets over Agrabah
7 - Armageddon: The Special Effects
8 - Disney Junior: Live on Stage
9 - Rock 'n' Roller Coaster: Starring Aerosmith
10 - Moteurs...Action! Stunt Show Spectacular
11 - Stitch Live!
12 - Art of Disney Animation
13 - The Twilight Zone: Tower of Terror
14 - Studio Tram Tour: Behind the Magic
15 - Ratatouille: The Adventure
16 - Toy Soldiers Parachute Drop
17 - Slinky Dog Zig Zag Spin
18 - RC Racer

24432969R00071

Printed in Great Britain
by Amazon